D0180236

Consumer
Reports

1,001
Helpful Hints

Consumer Reports

1,001 Helpful Hints

**The Editors of Consumer Reports
with Monte Florman**

**Consumer Reports Books
A Division of Consumers Union
Yonkers, New York**

Consumer Reports 1,001 helpful hints / the editors of Consumer Reports with Monte Florman.
    p.   cm.
    Rev. ed. of: 1,001 helpful tips, facts & hints from Consumer Reports. c1989.
    Includes index.
    ISBN 0-89043-847-1
    1. Consumer education.   I. Florman, Monte.   II. Consumer Reports. III. 1,001 helpful tips, facts & hints from Consumer Reports.
TX336.C654 1996
640'.41—dc20   96-5525
                                                      CIP

Design by Joseph DePinho

Page composition by Maggie Brenner

First printing, July 1996

This book is printed on recycled paper. ♻

Manufactured in the United States of America

Consumer Reports 1,001 Helpful Hints is a Consumer Reports Book published by Consumers Union, the nonprofit organization that publishes *Consumer Reports*, the monthly magazine of test reports, product Ratings, and buying guidance. Established in 1936, Consumers Union is chartered under the Not-for-Profit Corporation Law of the State of New York.

The purposes of Consumers Union, as stated in its charter, are to provide consumers with information and counsel on consumer goods and services, to give information on all matters relating to the expenditure of the family income, and to initiate and to cooperate with individual and group efforts seeking to create and maintain decent living standards.

Consumers Union derives its income solely from the sale of *Consumer Reports* and other publications. In addition, expenses of occasional public service efforts may be met, in part, by nonrestrictive, noncommercial contributions, grants, and fees. Consumers Union accepts no advertising or product samples and is not beholden in any way to any commercial interest. Its Ratings and reports are solely for the use of the readers of its publications. Neither the Ratings, nor the reports, nor any Consumers Union publications, including this book, may be used in advertising or for any commercial purpose. Consumers Union will take all steps open to it to prevent such uses of its material, its name, or the name of *Consumer Reports*.

Contents

Introduction 1

A

Air Bags, Facial Injuries 3
Air Conditioners 3
Airplane Seating Strategy 4
Apparel, Shopping Strategies 5
Aspirin 6
Automobile Batteries 7
Automobile Battery
    Booster Cables 9
Automobile Loans 10
Automobile Loans, Balloon 10

Automobile Rental Extras 11
Automobile Rental
    Fuel Charges 13
Automobile Repairs
    on the Road 13
Automobile Sales, Used Cars 14
Automobile Tires 14
Automobile Warranties 16
Automobile Washing
    and Polishing 17

B

Batteries 20
Bicycle Helmets 20
Bicycles 21
Bond Grades 23
Boom Boxes 23

Bread 24
Breadmakers 27
Bread Spreads 29
Burglar Alarms 30
Buying Advice, General 32

C

Caffeine 34
Calcium in the Diet 36
Calorie Budgeting 37
Camcorders 38
Cameras..................................38
Can Openers 39
Carbon Monoxide Detectors....40
CD Players.............................41
Cereal Prices..........................42
Chocolate Chip Cookies..........42
Christmas Trees......................44
Clothes Dryers 45

Coffee, Brewed 45
Coffee Beans.............................46
Coffeemakers............................46
Comforters 49
Common Cold 50
Computer Buying 50
Computer Printers 52
Condoms...................................53
Cordless Telephones 54
Credit Cards 55
Cribs and Crib Mattresses........58

D

Declaration of Independence....60
Dehumidifiers 60
Dehydration............................61
Depression/Holiday Blues........62
Dips and Chips 62

Dishwasher Detergents 63
Dishwashers 63
Doctors.....................................65
Door Locks 65
Drain Cleaning.........................67

E

Economic Statistics 68
Eggs 70
Electric Blankets
    and Mattress Pads................71
Electric Ranges 72
Energy Conservation 73

Exercise During the Day 76
Exercise During Winter............76
Exercise Machines....................77
Extended Warranties................81
Eyesight Damage......................82

F

Fast Food 83
Fat-Free Foods 84
Fats in the Diet 84
Fax Machines 85
Fiber in the Diet.....................87
Film 89
Fire Extinguishers...................90

Fish..93
Food Labeling...........................94
Food Mixers.............................95
Food Wraps and Containers......96
Fragrances 98
Furnace Efficiency....................99

G

Garage Door Openers 103
Garbage Bags 105
Garbage Disposers 106

Gas Ranges 109
Glue 111

H

Halogen Lamps 112
Hands, Smelly 112
Hazardous Waste at Home 112
Heartburn 114
Heaters, Portable 115

Herbal Supplements 116
Homeowner's Insurance 117
Home Theater 119
Hotel Security 120
Humidifiers 121

I

Ice Cream 123
Iced Tea 124
Impotence 124
Insect Repellents 125
Insomnia 127

Insurance Policy
   Cancellation 128
International Driving 128
Investing $50 or Less 129

J

Jack Stands 131

K

Kidney Stones 132

L

Laundry Detergents, Bleaches ..133
Laundry Detergents,
   Concentrated 133
Lawn Blowers 134
Lawn Mowers 134

Lipstick 136
Loans for the Self-Employed ...136
Long-Distance Calls 137
Loudspeakers 137
Luggage, Soft-Sided 138

M

Mail-Order Shopping 140
Microwave Ovens 140
Microwaving Produce 142
Milk, Acidophilus 142

Moisturizers, Facial 142
Mouthwash, Fluoridated 144
Muscle Sprains 144
Mutual Funds 145

N

Nail Care 147

O

Oranges and Orange Juice 148

P

Paints, Interior Latex 149
Peanut Butter 150
Peanuts 150
Pesticides in Baby Food 151

Pneumonia Vaccination 151
Pocket Knives 151
Power Drills............................152
Pressure Cookers 253

R

Receivers.................................154
Refrigerators 154
Remote Controls....................157

Repairing Appliances 158
Rollerblading...........................161

S

Safe-Deposit Box Insurance ...162
Salsa.......................................162
Saws, Saber 163
Screwdrivers 164
Shoes, Dress............................165
Shoes, Running 166
Shopping Channels on TV 167
Shopping Rights.....................168
Showerheads 170
Smoke Detectors 171
Smoking at 65 173
Soaps 173
Solvent Hazards 175

Soups 177
Spackling 179
Steam Irons 180
Stir-Frying...............................180
Stolen Check Liability............180
Strep Infection, Children.......181
Strollers 182
Sulfites in Wine.......................183
Sunscreens...............................183
Surge Suppressors
    for Computers 185
Sweaters...................................185
Swimmer's Ear........................186

T

Tampons and
Feminine Hygiene Pads.....187
Tape Decks 188
Teeth, Gum Disease 188
Teeth, Preventing Decay........189
Teeth, Sensitivity....................189
Telephone
Answering Machines.........190
Telephone Rates 192
Television Sets........................192
Thermostats, Energy-Saving....193

Time-Share Real Estate...........193
Toaster Oven–Broilers 194
Toasters...................................195
Toilet Tank, Water Savings.....195
Tomatoes.................................196
Toys and Games......................196
Trash Compactors 197
Treasury Securities..................198
Tuna Canned in Oil 199
Turkey.....................................199
TV/VCR Combinations..........201

V

Vacation Money.......................202
Vacation-Planning 204
Vacuum Cleaners 205
Variable Annuities...................206

Vegetable Nutrition.................206
Videocassette Recorders 207
Videotape 208
Vitamins..................................209

W

Warehouse Clubs 211
Washing Machines...................212
Weather Radios 212

Weather Stripping...................213
Windows, Replacement 215

Y

Yogurt.....................................217

Index 219

Acknowledgments

* *

The Editors of Consumer Reports Books would like to express their appreciation to the following individuals and their staffs at Consumers Union for reviewing the material contained in this book. They are Edward Groth III, Director, Technical Policy and Public Service; Thomas Deutsch, Assistant Director, Technical Operations; Robert Knoll, Testing Director, Auto Test; Bert Papenburg, Testing Director, Chemical & Textile; Alan Lefkow, Testing Director, Electronics; Constance Corbett, Testing Director, Foods; Mark Connelly, Testing Director, Appliances and Home Environment; and Donald Mays, Testing Director, Recreation & Home Improvement.

Introduction

Consumer Reports 1,001 Helpful Hints is a compendium of facts, tips, and advice on consumer matters covering a broad spectrum of information culled from past issues of *Consumer Reports* and other Consumers Union publications. This edition follows the format and organization of *1,001 Helpful Tips, Facts & Hints from Consumer Reports*, and includes practical and informative facts, buying advice, and general information on a range of products and services for your home, your car, your leisure time, your health, and your finances.

The marketplace for products and services, already huge and unwieldy, continues to become even broader, with advertising claims and selling pressure contributing to uncertainty and confusion in making buying decisions. Making informed decisions about spending your money is becoming more difficult than ever. Using this book, along with *Consumer Reports* and other Consumers Union publications, will help you to become better informed about energy conservation, hazardous household waste products, fat-free foods, automobile rental extras, investing $50 or less, and rollerblading.

And there's a lot more. You'll learn about shopping for a comforter, dealing with automobile repairs when you're driving a distance from home, shopping by mail or from TV shopping channels, and how to determine whether it's worth replacing your home's old windows or making other kinds of repairs around the house.

You'll find tips about buying perfume, features to look for in shoes for comfort or for running, the safety of insect repel-

1

lents you apply to the skin, and differences between photographic films.

By consulting the hints provided in this book, readers at a glance can learn how to save time, money, and energy. Written in easy-to-understand language, this book provides the essential information consumers need to shop wisely for the products and services that most impact their lives.

A

Air Bags, Facial injuries

There is a small but definite risk to the eye and the bones around the eye when an air bag inflates during a car crash. The risk is lessened if you're wearing a safety belt, and also if you wear nonshattering glasses. But those risks are significantly outweighed by the benefits of air bags, which are intended to save lives and often do.

Air Conditioners

Federal law requires appliance manufacturers to label air conditioners with an Energy Efficiency Rating (EER), a guide to energy consumption. The EER is figured by dividing the Btu per hour by the watts of power used. Other things—like room size and the air conditioner's capacity—being equal, a higher EER means lower energy consumption.

Cooling capacity. Know how much cooling capacity you'll need before heading for the stores. The table on page 4, developed by Carrier Corporation, gives a rough idea of the capacity needed.

Installation and maintenance. The easiest models to install (or service) have a slide-out chassis: First, the empty cabinet must be mounted in the window. (Large models with heavy innards come with brackets to anchor the cabinet.) Once that is done, the unit itself is simply slid in and any insulation or other accessories installed according to the instructions supplied.

COOLING CAPACITY

Room Area	Capacity
100 to 150 sq. ft.	5,000 Btu/hr.
150 to 250	6,000
250 to 300	7,000
300 to 350	8,000
350 to 400	9,000
400 to 450	10,000
450 to 550	12,000
550 to 700	14,000
700 to 1,000	18,000

Cleaning the filter is an important maintenance task, since filters clogged with dust from recirculating room air reduce efficiency and increase energy consumption. The filter should be inspected every week or so during the cooling season and washed or vacuumed according to the manufacturer's instructions. Cleaning and servicing is simplest if the filter slides out easily.

Airplane Seating Strategy

You can put up with even the worst airline seating if you're next to an empty seat. Here's how to increase your odds of sitting next to an empty:

On a wide-body plane, request an aisle seat in the center section. Middle seats in the center section are considered the least desirable, so they're the last to be assigned.

If most of the seats on a plane are in groups of three, one member of a couple will almost always be assigned to a middle seat. Couples can ask for an aisle and a window seat in a three-seat row. There's a good chance that the middle seat won't be assigned.

Several large airlines have reserved a section in coach for very-frequent-flier members of their frequent-flier programs. Those airlines say they assign middle seats in those sections only when planes are full. If you're a very-frequent flier, that's a big advantage. But if you're not, your odds of being in a middle seat or next to an occupied middle seat increase.

Apparel, Shopping Strategies

There are a number of ways to make your clothes-shopping experience more productive and perhaps more enjoyable.

For all shoppers

Know a store's return policy. For any store, bring clothes back with receipts and tags. But depending on the store, the return period can be as short as seven days.

Use bank credit cards, not store cards, if you don't always pay your bill in full. The interest charged with store cards may be more than twice as high as that charged on bank cards. On some nonapparel items, bank cards may offer warranties that store cards don't provide.

If possible, never choose a store credit on returned merchandise. Why let the store keep your money until the next time you're there?

If the store in which you're shopping has a catalog, you or a salesperson can call the catalog operation for items you can't find. Catalog inventory is sometimes larger and more diverse.

Don't buy a winter coat at full price. You can nearly always find what you want on sale, even in department stores. If it's July and you can't find a swimsuit, consider shopping at an outlet center or off-price store. These stores hold on to seasonal merchandise longer than do other types of retailers. So do many mail-order companies.

For sport shoppers

You'll need tags and receipts if your shopping pattern is to buy an item at one store, find the same thing elsewhere at a lower price, and then return the first item. If the jacket you bought last week goes on sale this week, some stores will refund the difference in price.

Don't go to an outlet store to browse. Rely on a shopping list. Chances are, you drove a distance to reach the outlet; if you go home with something you decide you don't want or need, you may not be able to return it. And even if you can, it could be a long way to travel just to get your money back. If you really want to browse, stick to a budget.

When time is short

If your schedule is tight, note that some stores schedule early-morning shopping hours during the holidays.

If you have a lot of gifts to buy and limited time, make an appointment with the personal shopper that some department stores offer. The shopper will make selections for you. But let the shopper know you won't budge beyond your budget.

Looking for bargains

Comparison shop. Department stores have the greatest variety, but other types of store may have better prices.

Concentrate on the price, not the percentage markdown on the label. The value you're getting now is what's crucial.

Consider private-label clothing. It can be of high quality, for less than you'd pay for a brand name.

Aspirin

Generic aspirin does the same thing as brand-name aspirin and is a lot cheaper. But sometimes generic aspirin (as well as brand-name aspirin) may have a strong odor when you open the bottle. A certain amount of vinegarlike smell is normal.

The smell comes from acetic acid, which is produced as all aspirin gradually breaks down. If the smell seems excessive, it's worth checking the expiration date on the label to be sure the aspirin is from fresh stock. Even new aspirin has some vinegary smell, but if the odor becomes too strong, the tablets should be discarded.

Automobile Batteries

When an automobile battery dies, you are often left stranded on the road. You have to get help from the nearest service station or auto center and settle for whatever the people there recommend.

You'll probably get a better battery at a better price—and save yourself aggravation—if you buy a new battery before the old one fails. The usual telltale sign of a weak battery is slow cranking of the starter motor, especially in cold weather. It's those sluggish starts that should prompt you to visit the service station or auto center.

If there aren't any obvious problems, the battery should be fully charged and a simple procedure known as a load test performed. A battery that's more than about four years old and is slow cranking will probably require replacement.

The fresher a car battery is when you buy it, the better. Unfortunately, manufacturers seldom make it easy to tell when the battery was made. The date code can appear on a sticker affixed to the battery or stamped on the case. It may be a string of letters and numbers, but in most cases all the information you need is in the first two characters—one a letter and one a digit. Most codes start with the letter, which represents the month: A for January, B for February, and so on. The digit indicates the year—6 for 1996. So, A-6 stands for January 1996; B-6 would represent February 1996.

Battery maintenance for long life

These steps will help ensure a long life for your battery:

- With a low-maintenance battery, check the level of the electrolyte—battery liquid—every month or so at first. Top off the battery cells beneath each vent cap with water as needed (distilled water, whenever possible) and replace the caps securely.

- Check the hold-down hardware that keeps the battery from vibrating. Vibration can shorten a battery's life.

- A deep discharge that leads to a dead battery, such as from inadvertently having left the headlights on, is not only inconvenient; it reduces a battery's lifetime, especially for a maintenance-free model. Keep a set of booster cables on hand for a jump start from another car, and be sure you know how to connect the cables properly—in the correct sequence and to the right terminals. (*See* Automobile Battery Booster Cables.)

- Neutralize the sulfuric acid that can damage battery terminals by washing the exposed metal cable parts and the battery terminals with a solution of baking soda and water.

- Batteries last longer if they're maintained as close to fully charged as possible. If you drive your car infrequently—no more than once every few weeks, say—and mostly for short distances, consider using a battery charger to keep the battery up to snuff.

- Sometimes, automotive battery problems aren't the battery's fault. If the battery is properly maintained but too weak to crank the engine, check the charging system and the alternator belt. If possible, go to a mechanic you trust; electrical components—especially batteries and alternators—are too often replaced unnecessarily.

Automobile Battery Booster Cables

The quickest way to get a car with a dead battery back on the road is usually to jump-start it with another car, using booster cables. Cables should be standard equipment for your car, especially if you live in a cold climate.

If winters are mild where you live, it's all right to buy by price alone, providing the cable clamps fit the battery configuration in your car.

Cold weather, however, calls for cables with thick (4- or 6-gauge) wire, which delivers the high current necessary to start a cold engine.

Jump-starting safely

Before you begin to attach cables, switch off the ignition and all electrical accessories in both cars, and make sure the two cars aren't touching.

1. Connect a positive (red) clamp to the disabled car's positive battery terminal; it's marked +, P, or Pos, and its battery lead is usually red in color.

2. Move to the healthy car and attach the other red clamp to its positive battery terminal.

3. Still at the boosting car, clip one negative (black) clamp to a nonmoving, unpainted metal part in the engine compartment. That is safer than attaching the clamp to the battery's negative terminal, as the owner's manual may recommend. Now start the boosting car and rev its engine. (Some cars, however, should not be running as they jump-start another vehicle; check the owner's manual.)

4. Finally, return to the disabled car and attach the other negative clamp, again to a suitable spot in the engine compartment.

The car should now start readily. If it doesn't, wait a few minutes and try again. After you're successful, remove the cables in the reverse order in which they were attached.

Automobile Loans

If you want to pay more than the required monthly payment on an automobile installment loan to reduce interest payments, you may wonder how you can be assured that the additional money will be applied to the principal.

If you have a simple interest loan, any overpayment will be applied directly to the principal. Your loan documentation should tell you what type of loan you have. If it is a simple interest loan, you will save money by prepaying the principal. But if the loan is not simple interest, paying off your loan early will not necessarily reduce your interest payments. To be sure no mistakes are made, you may want to attach a note to any additional payments or call the lender before you start making the larger payments. And, just to be prudent, you should check in with the lender again before you make your last payment to see what remaining balance you have.

Automobile Loans, Balloon

With a balloon loan you borrow enough money to finance the difference between the car's selling price and its expected value at the end of a set period, usually three or four years. At the end of that time, you must pay off the balance (the balloon), which may be a substantial sum. The monthly payment is lower because you aren't financing the entire value of the car. Before you enter such an arrangement, ask these questions: How will the value of the car be determined when the balloon is due?

And what interest rate would you have to pay if you choose to take out a new loan to pay off the balloon? All in all, the potential risks can easily outweigh any savings.

Automobile Rental Extras

Anyone who has rented a car is aware of many extras—items not quoted in or covered by the basic weekly rental rate—and limitations that can add substantially to the cost and nuisance of renting a car. Here are some of the worst offenders:

Advance reservations. Sometimes, the cheapest weekly rate requires you to reserve anywhere from one hour to 14 days in advance. Where required, the advance-reservation period is usually no more than one day. But some companies' rules for some locations require 7, 10, or even 14 days' notice.

Airport surcharges and local taxes. More and more airports and local authorities are adding fees and taxes to car-rental rates. Out-of-towners are a tempting target, since they can't vote against the local officials who apply the bite. Airport surcharges can run as high as close to 9 percent of the rental contract.

Such taxes don't usually vary by company. But sometimes, an off-airport car-rental office may be located in a local jurisdiction different from the airport's and therefore subject to slightly different local taxes. (You may be able to duck the airport add-on entirely if you don't use the rental company's shuttle bus to get to an off-airport rental office.)

Air ticket tie-in. Car-rental companies sometimes reserve their best rates for travelers arriving from out of town—local renters must pay more. To qualify for the rock-bottom rate, you must show your ticket for an air trip originating in some other city. There doesn't appear to be any consistency either by company or by location.

Child seat. Most car-rental companies charge a few dollars a

day for a child's seat—mandatory if you don't bring your own.
Collision-damage waiver. CDW is a waiver of the company's right to pursue for damage to the car you've rented while it's in your possession. It's grossly overpriced. Buy it only if your own auto insurance policy or your charge card doesn't cover you.

Driving record. More and more companies apparently check driving records before they'll rent prospects a car. If you have two or more recent moving violations on your record, ask if your record is acceptable when you reserve the car. If you wait until you arrive at the rental counter to find your record has been rejected, it may be too late to make alternate transportation arrangements.

Extra-day charge. If you keep a car on a weekly rental for an extra day, you're likely to be gouged. With most companies, the charge for an extra day is 20–25 percent of the weekly rental, rather than the 14 percent it would be if prorated.

Extra driver. One of the most annoying and least defensible of all car-rental charges is the requirement that anyone who drives the car, other than the person who signs the rental agreement, must pay extra. Such charges may be waived for spouses and business associates. However, these charges can vary by location, so you must ask each time to be sure.

Liability insurance. Supplementary liability insurance is available at something close to $10 per day. (Liability insurance covers you for damage you might cause to someone else or someone else's property.)

Rental companies have stopped providing any liability coverage in a few states. In other states, the companies generally provide only the minimum liability insurance that state law requires. That falls far short of what's needed to protect against a possible judgment for liability damages. But that doesn't mean you have to pay the daily charge. Adequate liability insurance is coverage that you need anytime you drive, not just when you rent a car. If you drive your own car, your own regular insurance may well cover you in a rented car. If it doesn't, you may have an extra "umbrella" liability policy that does.

If you don't have year-round liability insurance that covers you in a rented car, by all means buy the daily insurance. It may be overpriced, but it's a bargain compared with losing a lawsuit.

Automobile Rental Fuel Charges

Most major car-rental agencies ask if you'd like to pay for a full tank of gas when you take the car out, at a reasonable price for the fuel. The offer may seem attractive, but consider: Unless you return the car with an empty tank, whatever gas is left belongs to the rental company, who resells it to the next customer. The more economical choice is to pay for the gas you use: Take the car out with the full tank it is supposed to have and return it with the same full tank. That may cause some inconvenience during the rush of returning the car, depending on the accessibility of a gas station, but the tradeoff is saving some money.

Automobile Repairs on the Road

Some auto repair cheats target cars with out-of-state plates. Here are some of the more common repair scams:

Smoking alternator. The attendant empties an eyedropper of antifreeze on the hot alternator, making it smoke. You're sold a new alternator which, in reality, is your old one, disguised with quick-drying metallic paint.

Leaky radiator. The attendant jabs a small sharpened screwdriver into the radiator or hose. You're told you need a new radiator.

Leaky tire. Same method, to sell you a tire.

Defective shock absorber. While the car is raised on a lift, the attendant squirts oil on one of the shock absorbers and says the shock is leaking so badly that it (and its partner on the other side) should be replaced immediately.

Exploding battery. The attendant drops Alka-Seltzer tablets into the battery cells (assuming they're not sealed) and replaces the caps. Soon, a minor explosion blows off the caps—and you are paying for a new battery.

Loose spark-plug cable. You pay for a tune-up as the result of a cable that's been deliberately loosened.

"Short sticking." When checking the oil, an attendant pushes the dipstick in only partway so it registers a quart low. The "solution" is to add a quart of oil from an empty container.

The missing fuel cap. Avoid the disappearing fuel cap act and other scams by not leaving your vehicle unattended at a service station while you're traveling.

Automobile Sales, Used Cars

Years ago, when automakers unveiled their new models in the fall, prices on recent-model used cars declined. Today, manufacturers introduce new models throughout the year—often with few noticeable changes. So, used-car prices aren't affected as much by new-model introductions. Prices of used cars do tend to drop more in December and January, but that's because of reduced wintertime demand, not the start of a new year.

Automobile Tires

Some tires offer long tread life or a quiet and soft ride. Performance tires primarily offer grip. Whether the road is wet or dry, performance tires stop the car short, and they hang on in hard turns. They're not just for sporty cars. These tires can markedly improve even an ordinary sedan's braking.

Modern performance tires are available with designs that

seem to exact little or no penalty in ride comfort or noise. Performance tires do tend to wear more quickly than ordinary tires, but that's a reasonable price to pay for the added safety benefits they provide.

It can be tricky to distinguish a performance tire from other tires. Here's a rough guide to the terminology:

All-season tires. These are standard equipment on most sedans. They're designed to perform reasonably well under a variety of driving conditions—dry weather, rain, snow—without necessarily excelling in any one. Generally, these tires offer long tread life and good ride comfort.

Touring tires. A notch higher in performance, they put more emphasis on handling and cornering grip, with little loss in ride comfort and noise. Many of these tires are offered in T or H speed ratings, 118 mph and 130 mph, respectively.

All-season performance tires. This is a relatively new category of tire that not only carries performance characteristics but also is rated for all-season use. These tires have a speed rating of H (130 mph) and are also available in V or Z rating, which ups their speed to 149 and 168 mph respectively. These ratings do not mean that you have to drive that fast to benefit, but a high-speed rating generally indicates higher overall performance—a tire that grips unusually well and handles responsively.

Performance tires. These are often called "summer tires." They carry a high speed rating of at least H. They are designed for best handling and steering response but are not intended for use in snow.

Here are some tire maintenance tips.

- Check pressure monthly—after the car has sat for a couple of hours, so the tires are cold. Use the pressures listed on the driver's door or in the owner's manual.

- If the tread looks as if it is wearing unevenly, have the car's alignment checked.

- A bubble in the sidewall portends a blowout; replace the tire as soon as possible.

- Rotate the tires at least every 10,000 miles. However, the best advice is to follow the owner's manual or the tire manufacturer's recommendations. Rotation is the best way to extend the life of your tires. Rotation patterns vary; check the owner's manual.

- High speeds, wheel-spinning acceleration, hard cornering, and panic braking reduce tire life.

- If you can't straddle or steer around a pothole, brake hard—but release the pedal just before the tire drops into the pothole so it can roll through.

Automobile Warranties

The basic new-car warranty, which covers practically everything except wear parts (tires, wipers, brake pads, filters, and such), typically lasts three years or 36,000 miles, whichever comes first. A few makes, mostly with luxury nameplates, offer a basic warranty that lasts four years or 50,000 miles.

Except for emergencies, warranty work is normally performed by an authorized dealer, but it doesn't have to be the one that sold you the car. You can have routine maintenance, such as oil changes, performed by a garage or other repair facility without jeopardizing your warranty, as long as you keep service records and the work is done properly.

Most foreign automakers and a few upscale domestic ones cover the drivetrain (the engine and transmission) a year or two longer than the basic warranty does. In the last few years, "corrosion" warranties have become fairly standard. Surface rust isn't covered, but if a body panel rusts through, it's repaired or replaced at no charge. Rust-through coverage usually lasts five to seven years and 100,000 or more miles.

Roadside assistance is a fairly new warranty feature. If your car breaks down, if you lock yourself out, or if you run out of fuel, you call a toll-free number for help. Often, roadside assistance is comprehensive and free regardless of the trouble. The terms vary. In most cases, towing is free only if a warranted part caused the breakdown. Towing may not be free if the car was vandalized or if there was a collision.

According to federal law, automakers must warrant all emissions-related equipment—several dozen parts from the intake manifold to the tailpipe—for two years or 24,000 miles. Some emissions-related components, like the catalytic converter and electronic emissions-control units, are covered for eight years or 80,000 miles. California requirements differ.

An extended warranty is usually nothing more than over-priced breakdown insurance. Coverage may not start until after the manufacturer's warranty expires. An extended service warranty might make sense for a car brand and model with a demonstrably poor reliability record.

Automobile Washing and Polishing

A couple of generations ago, people may have waxed their cars with carnauba wax (from a Brazilian palm tree) or beeswax. However, most modern waxes are petroleum-based, which tends to make them cheaper and easier to use. Other ingredients in today's car polishes are solvents or petroleum distillates, whose fumes make it necessary to wax a car outdoors.

As for paint, the metal body of any car made before the early 1980s was coated with a primer, then a thick layer of colored paint. In many newer cars, the primer is topped by a thin layer of colored paint, then a thin layer of clear paint designed to make the finish glossier, more durable, and slower to oxidize. But even the new paints oxidize eventually. Every new car will someday lose its glow and succumb to sun, ice, salt, tree sap, and other environmental assaults. Wax may help slow the process or make a noticeable difference if weathering of the finish has already started.

Washing before waxing

Frequent washing removes dirt from a car's finish before it can do lasting damage. Before you wash, consider the weather. Never wash in direct sunlight or when the paint is hot to the touch. That can soften the paint, making it more vulnerable to abrasion or water spots on the finish. If sunshine is unavoidable, wash either early or late in the day, when the sun's rays are less intense.

Here's the right way to wash:

• Flush away loose dirt by hosing down the whole car. Be sure to direct the spray especially to the undercarriage and wheel wells.

• Remove any heavy deposits of tree sap or road tar with a soft cotton rag that you've dampened with mineral spirits or a cleaner specifically designed for the job. Rinse the area immediately.

• While the car is still wet, use a lambs-wool mitt or soft cotton cloth (avoid synthetic fabrics or brushes, which can scratch) to apply a mix of water and detergent. A cleaner especially formulated for cars should spare existing wax. It is uncertain whether dishwashing detergent is too harsh for a car's finish.

• Wash from the top of the car down, so you don't have to clean lower areas repeatedly. Rinse the mitt or cloth often and the car periodically, before the suds can dry. Check the finish for beads of water. If the beads are bigger than a quarter or if the water forms sheets, it's time to wax.

• After the last rinse, dry with a soft cotton towel or genuine chamois.

If you opt to take the car to a car wash instead of doing the job yourself, choose one with a brushless system, which won't scratch.

B

Batteries

If you use AAA, AA, C, D, or the 9-volt size of battery, the alkaline variety is a good all-purpose choice, especially if you don't want to fuss with a battery charger. There's little difference in battery life from one brand to another. Alkaline batteries have a long storage life, so you can stock up on one of the widely sold brands.

Heavy-duty batteries may be adequate for low-drain uses—in a wall clock or remote control, for instance—but not much else. Even then, their small price advantage over alkalines isn't worth nearly what you will sacrifice in hours of running time.

In devices that run on two or more batteries, replace all the batteries at once. Mixing old and new batteries doesn't give the best results. *Nickel-cadmium batteries.* Rechargeable batteries of this type offer considerable savings to people who use lots of batteries. But rechargeables generally last only a fraction as long as alkaline batteries—and they die abruptly. You must also buy a recharger. The need for recharging at an inopportune time can be a nuisance unless you keep a charged set of batteries within easy access.

Bicycle Helmets

Most helmets adhere to one or more voluntary safety standards set by the American National Standards Institute (ANSI), the Snell Memorial Foundation (named after the race-car driver), and the American Society for Testing and Materials (ASTM).

No cyclist should take even a short ride without wearing a bicycle helmet. Any helmet that meets Snell, ANSI, or ASTM safety standards should offer adequate protection, provided it's fitted correctly.

A typical helmet should have a thin plastic shell covering a plastic foam liner; an adjustable chin and front and rear side straps; pads in various thicknesses that can be repositioned; a side-squeeze quick-release buckle; fitting instructions; and a free lifetime crash replacement.

Children and helmets. Although helmet laws obviously help, parents still bear the primary responsibility for encouraging helmet use and safe riding.

Here are some cycling safety tips:

- Set a good example by wearing a helmet yourself whenever you ride a bike.

- Don't buy a helmet that's too large, thinking the child will grow into it. A helmet that's too big is likely to roll off, reducing its ability to protect.

- Adjust a child's helmet so it fits snugly and correctly. Readjust the fit as the child grows.

- Discourage children from riding at times when accidents are most prevalent: dawn, dusk, and at night.

- Encourage a child to ride on bike paths or in other low-traffic areas.

Bicycles

Casual bikes. The hybrid bike is for plain folks, not racers or off-roaders. It's lighter and easier to ride on pavement than a mountain bike, and more stable and shock-absorbing than a road bike when jumping curbs and negotiating off-road trails. With their relatively wide tires, hybrids are suitable for, say, a gravel road or a dirt track. Like mountain bikes, hybrids have powerful cantilever brakes, a wide range of gears, a fairly comfortable saddle, and flat handlebars for upright seating. Even the lowest-priced models are higher in quality (and price) than the cheapest mountain bikes.

If a particular bike has most, but not all, of the components you want, ask about having some of them changed. Bike stores may be willing to switch the shifter, saddle, and other components to suit you. If the replacements are a similar price, the switches may be made at no charge.

These bikes come in at least four frame sizes. It's important to get the right size; a frame that's too small or too large will feel uncomfortable and handle poorly. If the frame is too large, it will also be heavier than necessary.

Things to expect when you buy a midpriced ($350–$450) hybrid bike: Smooth shifting, steady handling, and good shock absorption on pavement; dirt/moisture seals on crank and hubs; raising and lowering the handlebars to affect front-brake settings; quick-release levers for wheels and seat post, and front-wheel retention device; frames and forks made all or partly of chromium-molybdenum ("chromoly") steel; cantilever brakes with levers that are adjustable for hand size.

Mountain bikes. Most mountain bikes never get near a mountain. Despite names that suggest rough riding, these bikes are primarily pedaled on regular roads, where their cushiony tires and upright handlebars offer a comfortable ride.

Special needs may help you narrow your selection. If you're shopping for a youngster (or a small adult), make sure a bike's brake levers can be adjusted to accommodate small hands. If you live in a hilly region, avoid bikes whose gearing isn't low enough for steep climbs or high enough for rapid descents. If you often ride in dusty conditions, sealed bearings in the crank and hubs may be particularly helpful in reducing maintenance.

Bond Grades

Here are the bond-rating grades used by Standard & Poor's, one of the major bond-rating services (other bond-rating services use their own designations):

- AAA is the highest rating. It means the issuers of the bonds have the greatest ability to pay interest and to repay principal, in the judgment of the rating service.

- AA indicates the next-highest ability to meet obligations to bondholders.

- A is for bonds from companies that have good credit ratings but that could be affected by economic downturns.

- BBB indicates only an adequate capacity to meet obligations. Adverse economic conditions could lead to default.

- BB means a speculative bond with substantially more risk.

- B means a bond is among the most risky junk bonds.

- B– means a speculative junk bond or possibly a bond that is infrequently traded.

- CCC, CC, C, D ratings refer to bonds that are in, or about to go into, default.

Boom Boxes

In price and performance, boom boxes fill the niche between a clock radio or walkabout CD player and a stereo minisystem. Their portability and simple design make them suitable as a youngster's first stereo system, for college-bound students, and for adults who want a backup to their main system.

Early boom boxes sounded much like good table radios. They

usually had AM/FM radio and a single tape deck. In time, the box acquired a second deck for easy tape-to-tape copying; then a CD player was added to the mix. Today, all but the least expensive boom boxes have a CD player, and some boxes even let you play more than one disc.

A big boom box weighs in at about 15 to 22 pounds with batteries. It has detachable speakers you position for the best stereo effect. Small boxes weigh half as much as larger ones and generally have attached speakers. They don't have the ability to reproduce sound that is faithful to the original.

With CD boom boxes, the choice boils down to this: Do you want good sound and a hefty box or so-so sound and a box you can take anywhere? The big models sound nearly as good as decent stereo minisystems, but their size makes them less suitable than smaller boxes for a day at the beach.

Bread

Bread has had a reputation for being fattening. In fact, bread is a good source of nutrients and has very little fat and relatively few calories. Some manufacturers make special "low-fat" or "fat-free" claims, but what they are simply stating is true of yeast breads in general: They're only as fattening as the butter or mayonnaise you smear on top.

Bread without any topping is high in energy-producing complex carbohydrates and contains fiber, protein, B vitamins, iron, and other vitamins and minerals. Whole-grain breads, which include the grain's germ and bran, also supply copper, magnesium, and zinc, and have more fiber than other breads.

Bread really *is* the staff of life—or at least it should be. The government's food-guide pyramid, describing a healthful daily diet, recommends 6–11 servings of bread and other carbohydrates (potatoes, grains, rice, etc.) every day. But Americans eat only a little more than two slices of bread a day (one slice equals a serving). White bread is by far the favorite, followed by whole-wheat, rye, and offshoots like rolls, pita, English muffins, and croissants.

White bread. An excellent white bread should taste distinctly of grain and have a slight yeast flavor. It may be slightly sweet. It must not have a musty, moldy, or chemical taste. The grain of the bread should be even, with no large air pockets, and moderately dense. Its texture may range from somewhat crumbly (but less crumbly than a corn muffin) to slightly stretchy, as in good Italian bread.

Whole wheat. An excellent whole-wheat bread should taste of baked whole wheat—a combination of distinct nutty and less pronounced haylike flavors. There may be a touch of caramelized flavor reminiscent of brown sugar or molasses, and the bread may be very slightly bitter or astringent. Whole-wheat flour generally produces a bread that's denser than white; wheat bits or berries may make the texture rougher.

Rye. An excellent rye bread should have a moderate grain flavor that is a combination of baked wheat and rye. It should have a touch of sourness. If the bread has caraway seeds, their flavor should be distinct but not overpowering. The texture should resemble that of whole-wheat bread, although it shouldn't seem as rough. Caraway seeds should add a slight crunch.

Nutrition

As a rule, a slice of commercially baked bread has one gram or less of fat, two to three grams of protein, negligible cholesterol, and one to two grams of fiber. (Larger slices of bread made at home in a breadmaker will have more of these nutrients.) Whole-wheat breads have slightly more protein than white or rye, and about twice as much fiber. (Still, it takes three or more slices of whole-grain bread to provide as much fiber as you get from a bowl of high-fiber cereal.)

If you look to bread as a source of dietary fiber, choose a whole-grain bread and be sure to eat a lot of it. If you use bread only as a way to keep your hands clean while eating a sandwich, you might as well choose by price.

Ounce for ounce, calories are about the same for most breads; slice by slice, the calorie count differs, because some slices are bigger or denser than others. Most white breads and ryes have around 60 to 80 calories per slice (an oversize slice from a breadmaker may have close to 130 calories); most whole-wheat breads have about 50 to 105 calories.

White and whole-grain "light" breads may have only 40 calories per slice. Manufacturers cut back on calories by slicing bread thinner, letting the dough rise more so the bread is airier, or adding fiber, which is indigestible and therefore adds no calories.

In losing calories, bread also loses taste. If you compensate for their mediocre taste by spreading on another knifeload of peanut butter, of course, you've lost the main advantage light bread offers.

The best bread is likely to be the kind you make at home—even in a breadmaker. That's not surprising: Whereas home bakers generally stick to basics like flour, milk, yeast, salt, and butter, commercial bakers often add ingredients—to promote longer shelf life or create an airier texture—that home bakers haven't even heard of. For example:

Gluten. Flour protein that may be added to improve the dough's stretching and rising.

Sugar. Helps start fermentation. Affects the crust's color and taste. Usually appears on labels as corn syrup, brown sugar, molasses, or honey.

Milk or whey. Improves nutritional quality and contributes to flavor and crust color.

Fat or oil. An optional ingredient, usually added in small amounts. Increases a loaf's volume and makes the bread more tender. May be soybean, cottonseed, or canola oil.

Dough enhancers. For instance, mono- and diglycerides, lecithin, sodium and calcium stearoyl-2-lactylate, propylene glycol, and azodicarbamide. These tongue-twisters are there to strengthen dough and facilitate rising. Some also soften the bread and help it stay fresh longer.

Calcium and ammonium sulfate and monocalcium phosphate. Sometimes labeled "yeast nutrients," they make the yeast do its job faster.

Calcium propionate or vinegar. Preservatives that inhibit the formation of mold and thus prolong shelf life.

Bread dating. It's hard to estimate the freshness of bread in stores. Some packages are stamped with "sell by" dates, others with "fresh through" dates; some list dates with no further explanation. National and regional brands may be stamped with dates almost a week away, whereas dates on supermarket brands are often just two or three days away. One explanation is that some national brands are taken off the shelves a few days before the date stamped on the package and sold at a discount in bakery-outlet shops.

To keep bread fresh, store it in a cool, dry place. That place shouldn't be the refrigerator. Although refrigeration slows mold growth, it hastens the crystallization of starch, which is what makes bread stale. If you won't be eating the bread within a few days, keep it in the freezer, where it should stay fresh for up to three months if properly wrapped. If a loaf does get stale, refresh it by covering it with a slightly dampened cloth and heating it in a warm oven.

Breadmakers

A breadmaker combines a food mixer and a mini-oven in one package. A motor-driven paddle in the bottom of the pan rotates to knead the dough, stops to let the dough rise, then sometimes repeats the process before the oven heats up to bake the bread, also in the same pan.

Depending on the brand, loaves may be round, square, or rectangular. The loaves are often taller than they are wide. A regular-loaf breadmaker takes about three to four cups of flour and makes a white bread that typically weighs about 1¼ pounds, yielding 10 to 14 thick, large slices.

A breadmaker isn't human. It doesn't measure ingredients or check that the yeast is fresh. It doesn't remember to put the kneading paddle in place, or check to see if the power is turned on, or remove the bread before it sits in the machine too long, getting soggy with condensation. For these tasks, the baker is still responsible.

A breadmaker isn't sensitive. An experienced chef, kneading by hand, may know when sticky dough needs extra flour because of humidity in the air or because the flour itself has absorbed moisture.

A breadmaker isn't flexible. With each step fixed in computer memory, you won't get the same variety of texture from loaf to loaf that you can get when you make bread by hand. And because each model is programmed differently, certain machines may not take well to certain recipes. In such cases, because you can't adjust the machine, you must adjust the ingredients.

Tips on the process

Basic breadmaking is the interaction of yeast, flour, water, salt, and often sugar. In the presence of lukewarm water and carbohydrates, the yeast multiplies rapidly and produces carbon dioxide. The carbon dioxide expands the gluten strands in the flour, making the dough rise. How far and how fast depends a lot on how much yeast, liquid, sugar, and salt there are. For a better loaf next time, here are some adjustments you can try:

Low-riser. This may mean you've used old yeast, too little water, or water that was too hot or too cold (hot kills yeast activity; cold slows it). Try again with fresh yeast and water that is lukewarm, and perhaps increase the water if the dough seems dry. If your goal is a whole-grain bread, you may need to substitute bread flour for some of the whole-wheat or rye flours. It is more difficult to get a bread with whole-grain flour to rise because the gluten in such flours isn't as strong.

High-rise (or collapsed) loaf. You may have added too much yeast or water. Experiment with less of those ingredients next time. Or try a little less sugar. A small-to-moderate amount of sugar feeds the yeast, making the dough rise faster. (A lot of sugar, as used in sweet dough, acts as an inhibitor.) Sometimes a dough rises too much before a bread starts to bake, the gluten strands of the flour become thin and weak, and carbon dioxide escapes. When that happens, the bread might rise and collapse, and the loaf will have a flat or sunken top.

Crumbly, airy loaf. More salt might help. Salt slows the rising of the dough and gives the bread a more even texture. If sodium is a concern and you want to bake with a minimum amount of it, try cutting the amount of yeast, too. (Conversely, if you add too much salt, the dough won't rise enough and the bread will be heavy and small.)

Bread Spreads

According to standards set by the U.S. Department of Agriculture and the Food and Drug Administration, butter and margarine must be at least 80 percent fat by weight. A tablespoonful of each has about 100 calories and 11 grams of fat. Butter is made from cream, milk, or both, and may contain salt, coloring, or both. Margarine is generally made from vegetable oil and may include water, milk, preservatives, and assorted other ingredients.

With margarine no longer much cheaper than butter and its

nutritional advantage less clear than once thought, margarine users have been defecting to butters and spreads. In response, manufacturers have reduced the amount of vegetable oil in their margarines, thereby turning them into spreads.

Light butter is made of the usual cream and milk but adds water and skim milk or other milk products to cut in half the calories and fat of regular butter. It also contains nondairy ingredients that add flavor and help hold it together.

Whipped butter is regular butter with air beaten into it. It is therefore less dense than the unwhipped type and, per tablespoon, has less fat and fewer calories.

Other butterlike products, including *diet margarine*, are known as *spreads*. Some spreads are made from vegetable oil and use water to displace fat. Certain spreads, called *blends*, contain not only vegetable oil but also milk fat in the form of butter, cream and skim milk, or sweet cream buttermilk.

Spreads may be promoted as more healthful than butter or margarine. Many are lower in calories and fat, but how much varies greatly from product to product.

Some vegetable-oil spreads are also advertised as lacking dietary cholesterol, but that's an empty claim. For one thing, all vegetable-oil products are free of cholesterol. For another, the cholesterol that finds its way into the arteries is affected much more by dietary saturated fat than by dietary cholesterol. It's the saturated fat in butter and other dairy products—and in red meat and many processed foods—that might do you in.

Burglar Alarms

Here are some basic steps to take in any home, even one that has a burglar alarm:

• Make would-be intruders think someone is home. Set up timers to control lights when you're away.

- Stop newspaper and mail deliveries for vacations. Make arrangements to have the lawn mowed (or the snow shoveled) while you're away.

- Keep an eye on neighbors' houses, and ask them to watch yours. If possible, leave a telephone number where you can be reached.

- If you do face an intruder, don't be a hero. Your life matters more than your property.

A house protected by a burglar alarm (or a home security system, as the fancier alarms are dubbed) is at least three times less likely to be burglarized than a house without an alarm. When burglars do break into an alarm-guarded house, they tend to get away with less than half the loot taken from an unguarded home.

Although a burglar alarm may confer peace of mind, it may not always be worth the expense. A do-it-yourself system may cost around $500. A professionally installed system can easily cost $1,000 to more than $3,000. Yet the average loss from a burglary is only around $1,000, and at least part of the loss is usually covered by insurance.

A home security system can also be a nuisance. Every time you go in or out, you must arm or disarm the alarm, and you have to think before you open doors or windows.

Details

If you want an alarm system, you need to decide first between a wired and a wireless system. A wired system has strategically placed sensors physically linked to a central control unit. With a wireless system, the sensors typically include a minuscule transmitter to communicate with the central control. The choice of a wired or wireless system largely depends on whether you want to handle the installation yourself or hire a professional.

A professionally installed system is usually armed and disarmed from a keypad, which you program to accept an access code.

Most wireless do-it-yourself systems have relatively simple controls and only a few operating options. The typical system can be armed and disarmed with a remote control. Simple enough, but equally simple for anyone else who gets the remote. Here are a few control features:

Away. This allows you about 30 seconds to exit after arming the alarm, or to disarm it when you enter.

Home or night. This setting, found on some systems, disables all interior motion detectors, so you can walk freely around the house.

Panic or emergency. A panic button sounds the alarm instantly, even if the system isn't armed. With a wired system, you must get to the central control panel to press the panic button (unless you order a separate switch or a remote control). With a wireless model, the panic button or its equivalent is on the remote control.

Buying Advice, General

It makes sense for consumers to develop a kind of philosophy about how and when to buy—and not to buy. Here are some questions you might ask yourself and some comments to help guide you.

Can that product be repaired rather than replaced? Maybe an appliance or a piece of electronic equipment can be fixed economically. If you choose to replace a product that still works, can you give the old one to someone who can use it, instead of throwing it away?

Do I truly need that new or pricey product? Advertisers have mastered every conceivable technique to get you to agree to a sale. Try to master techniques that help you say "No." If you really need to buy a new product, more-expensive versions aren't necessarily better.

Have I sought the best price? Sizable savings are available if you comparison shop.

Instead of buying, can I borrow, share, or rent? Power tools can be rented, baby furnishings recycled, gardening equipment shared with a neighbor. Car-pooling not only reduces costs, it helps reduce fuel consumption and the environmental damage caused by auto emissions.

Can I avoid more debt? Credit-card interest charges are high, well above other interest rates. Pay cash when you can, or spend little enough so that you can pay the full credit-card bill when it arrives in the mail.

Can I replace a private expenditure with a public one? You are already paying taxes to support essential public benefits. Choose public transportation, when available. Borrow books, magazines, videos, and music from the library. For children, this can be the start of a worthwhile lifetime habit.

C

Caffeine

Six ounces of most brewed coffees contain about 100 milligrams of caffeine, give or take 30 milligrams. That compares with about 50 to 90 milligrams of caffeine for most instant coffees. Contrary to what some dark-roast drinkers believe, a strong-tasting brew isn't necessarily one that's high in caffeine; if anything, a dark-roasted coffee supplies less caffeine, since more of the stimulant is driven off by heat when the beans are roasted.

Even the same product brewed the same way can vary appreciably; caffeine can differ by up to 50 percent from one sample to another.

If you want to avoid all caffeine in coffee—or just cut back—you can choose either decaffeinated coffee or reduced-caffeine coffee, the so-called "half-caf." (A cup of brewed decaf usually contains no more than 5 milligrams of caffeine. A cup of half-caf has about 50 milligrams.) Both kinds of caffeine-reduced coffee rely on decaffeinating green coffee beans before they are roasted.

Some decaf coffee drinkers have been concerned about the solvent methylene chloride, which was often used in the decaffeination process. (The chemical produced cancer in some tests on laboratory animals.) Coffee processors now use other decaffeination procedures. One of those alternatives is "indirect" decaffeination. Beans are soaked in plain water, which dissolves caffeine; the *water* is decaffeinated, then returned to the beans to try to restore flavors that might have leached out. Other processors use the solvent ethyl acetate, a natural component of some fruits, which lets them call their coffees "naturally decaffeinated." In the Swiss Water Process, activated charcoal is used to remove caffeine from the liquid the beans have soaked in. Another technique uses liquid carbon dioxide to do the job.

In fact, methylene chloride probably never posed any risk to coffee drinkers (although processes that don't use solvents may be better for the environment). Any solvent residue that remains on green coffee beans is driven off during roasting.

Regardless of the process used, decaffeination necessarily takes away some coffee taste. Decaffeinated regular-roast coffees tend to lack the subtle aroma of first-rate coffee. Decaf may also have a cereal taste and a slightly "cooked" character—all betraying the beans' extra processing.

Health risks

The mild lift provided by a cup or two of coffee can turn into anxious overstimulation after the day's fourth or fifth cup—or sooner in those who are particularly sensitive to caffeine. And caffeine creates dependence; coffee drinkers who are deprived of their daily dose may suffer headaches, tiredness, anxiety, and an impaired ability to perform physical tasks.

It is clear that caffeine is not innocuous. It acts powerfully on the mind and body but rarely poses a serious risk. As with most things in life, moderation is the key—and that's especially important for certain groups of those who consume caffeine.

Given some evidence associating caffeine and miscarriages, it makes sense for pregnant women (and perhaps women planning to become pregnant) to heed the U.S. Food and Drug Administration (FDA) advisory urging pregnant women to cut back on or give up the consumption of caffeine.

People with high blood pressure or those with an irregular

heartbeat should check with their doctors about consuming caffeine, since the drug can worsen both conditions.

Caffeine and digestion. Coffee prompts the stomach to secrete more gastric acid. Those who suffer from ulcers or frequent acid indigestion should avoid all coffee, including decaffeinated.

Caffeine in products other than coffee. The FDA and soft drink and instant coffee manufacturers advise that certain products contain the following amounts of caffeine:

PRODUCTS THAT CONTAIN CAFFEINE

	Average	Range
Drip-brewed coffee	100 mg.	70–215 mg
Instant coffee	70	35–169
Tea, U.S. brands	50	25–110
Cocoa	5	2–25
Mountain Dew (12 oz.)	54	
Coca-Cola (12 oz.)	46	
Dr. Pepper (12 oz.)	41	
Pepsi-Cola (12 oz.)	35	
Dark chocolate (1 oz.)	20	5–35
Milk chocolate (1 oz.)	6	1–15
Vivarin tablet	200	
No Doz tablet	100	
Excedrin	65	
Anacin	32	

Calcium in the Diet

A 1993 editorial in the *Journal of the American Medical Association* suggested that women, in particular, should double or triple their average daily intake of calcium. Such an increase may lower the risk of bone damage (osteoporosis) that occurs as part of the aging process.

Even a diet rich in calcium will probably fall short of the 1,000 or 1,500 milligrams of calcium a day (depending on age) recommended by the National Institutes of Health. Extra calcium is available in a variety of supplements.

Buy supplements by price. Choose calcium carbonate—it's by far the cheapest form. Look for an economical large bottle; you don't have to worry about the product losing its potency. If you want only 200 or so milligrams per pill, consider the antacids Tums or Rolaids.

Calorie Budgeting

Here's a way to estimate how many calories you can consume each day without gaining or losing weight.

Start with your weight in pounds. Multiply it by 10 if you're a woman, by 11 if you're a man. That yields your basic metabolic requirement. Then decide which of the following four categories best describes your highest level of regular exercise, and select the corresponding activity factor.

AMOUNT OF EXERCISE

Activity Level	*Activity Factor*
Sedentary	1.40
Light (housework, cooking, short stroll)	1.60
Moderate (brisk swimming or walking)	1.70
Strenuous (heart-pounding exercise)	1.85

Multiply your metabolic requirement by your activity factor to get your approximate daily calorie budget.

Camcorders

Camcorder prices have come down, and quality has improved. Even the plainest camcorder can produce good pictures in ample light. A 12:1 zoom lens is typical, and increasing numbers of models come with a color viewfinder, remote control, and special picture effects.

Compact camcorders are the most prevalent; the two types, 8mm and VHS-C, use different tapes. "High-band" versions—S-VHS-C and Hi8—provide sharper pictures in their high-band mode, which requires special higher-priced tapes. To get the most from high-band formats, get a TV with S-video input.

Compact machines are small, light, and easy to carry. Eight-mm models can record for up to two hours on one tape, and they have the potential for better sound quality than regular (non–hi-fi) VHS or VHS-C. The main advantage of VHS-C is easy playback. The 30-minute cassette (90 minutes at slow speed) fits an adapter to play in any VHS VCR. With 8mm, you play the tape from the camcorder or copy it to a VHS tape.

Cameras

Nearly all compact 35mm cameras include a built-in electronic flash and can load, advance, and rewind the film for you. They span a wide range of capabilities and prices, such as the following:

Nonzoom, fixed exposure. Fairly wide-angle lens. No exposure controls. This type is the low end of "point and shoot." Best suited for photos in bright light. These cameras don't perform well in close-ups and must use flash except in bright daylight. Approximate cost: $25 to $65.

Nonzoom, autoexposure. Fairly wide-angle lens. Automatic exposure control. The majority have autofocus. Well suited for snapshots; not as good as zoom-lens cameras for close-ups. Approximate cost: $60 to $170.

Medium zoom, autoexposure. Limited, although still useful, zoom range—generally 35mm to 70mm.

Autofocus and autoexposure. Suited for any type of photographs. Approximate cost: $140 to $385.

Long zoom, autoexposure. Wide range of focal lengths—generally about 38mm to 115mm. Autofocus and autoexposure. This type tends to have features of various kinds. Approximate cost: $180 to $320.

Other considerations

Spending more puts you in the realm of single-lens reflex (SLR) cameras—bigger and bulkier but more versatile. They can take many different lenses, and the reflex viewfinder provides accurate framing, even for tight close-ups.

Another advantage of most SLR cameras: Most allow you the option of adjusting exposure and focus manually. Thus you can make some creative decisions yourself—for example, to choose a faster shutter speed or a higher f-stop when you want to reduce blur or increase depth of field. But those advantages are mostly for serious photographers, those who've mastered the medium and constantly explore its limits.

Selling prices of SLR autofocus camera bodies alone range from about $300 to $850, and a zoom lens can add another $150 to $450. By comparison, a good compact camera with a zoom lens costs about $150 to $300. For most camera buyers, a compact is the camera of choice; a fancy SLR may provide more status than additional useful function.

Can Openers

Here are the majority of the choices in can openers:

Hand-held manual. Most are of the pliers-type design and have a gear-driven cutting wheel. Hand-held manual openers are typically made of metal, with handles covered in plastic or vinyl.

A bottle opener is usually built into one of the handles. Most rust if washed in a dishwasher.

Wall-mounted manual. These conveniently swing out of the way when not in use, folding up close to the wall or cabinet. They generally work well but may release cans somewhat reluctantly, which can cause spills.

Electric countertop. Most operate automatically: They pierce the lid, turn the can, and shut off on their own. There should be an easily removable, washable cutting head; it's probably best washed and dried by hand—to prevent rusting in the dishwasher. Some countertop models are tall enough to open tall cans; all can be moved to the edge of the counter to do so. Be careful, however, some may be tippy. This is the easiest type to use if your hand function is limited.

Under-cabinet electric. These don't take any counter space and attach easily under cabinets (they come with the necessary hardware for mounting). Under-cabinet models' cutting assembly is similar to that found on countertop models. Any of these openers should be able to handle tall cans.

Carbon Monoxide Detectors

A carbon monoxide (CO) detector is most important in homes that have a fuel-fired hot-air furnace or space heater, a wood stove, or a fireplace—common household sources of high levels of carbon monoxide. And a detector is doubly valuable if your house is also tightly weather-sealed. In an airtight house, there's a greater likelihood of the furnace's being starved for combustion air, increasing the incomplete burning that produces CO. There's also a higher risk of the backdrafts that can send CO-laden exhaust back down the furnace or fireplace flue and into the home.

Any home with a fuel-burning appliance or fireplace should

have at least one CO detector, ideally in a hallway or sleeping area. These detectors can reduce the toll of at least 200 yearly accidental deaths from CO poisoning and 5,000 emergency room admissions.

The real toll is very likely higher, since many of the symptoms of CO poisoning—dizziness, nausea, vomiting, fatigue—are mistaken for the flu or another illness.

Look for an alarm that stops automatically within minutes when the air is cleared of CO; manual hush or reset button to silence the alarm briefly in the presence of CO; digital display or warning light; light to indicate power is on; horn that sounds a loud alarm; test button to verify that the detector is working; with a plug-in model, a power cord at least six feet long; and on battery-powered models, a battery/sensor pack that lasts a few years.

Detection cards. Carbon monoxide detection cards that you stick to a wall have a sensor "spot" that's supposed to change color in response to CO. Even a card that works as it should is of limited use, since there's no alarm to alert you to a high CO level; you have to look at the spot. Since most people who die from CO poisoning are overcome while sleeping, cards aren't really effective by their very design.

CD Players

CD players, even inexpensive ones, sound superb. Many features are standard: remote control, track programming, shuffle play, a display that tells you what track is playing and its elapsed time. Among extra features that genuinely add to a player's value are a track keypad on the console; a calendar display that shows clearly the tracks on the disc being played; a memory buffer that shortens the gaps between tracks; and various ways of making it easier to tape music from a disc.

Components for a home audio system come in single-play

and carousel- and magazine-changer versions. You can also play CDs in portable versions.

Changers can be had for little more than single-play machines. Between the two multidisc types, carousel changers have reliability and easy loading in their favor; magazine changers use six-disc magazines that also work in some car players. With portables, choose a bare-bones model for low price.

Cereal Prices

It costs more to advertise and sell a box of brand-name cereal than to manufacture it. One consequence of this phenomenon is that the price of cereal has outpaced the consumer price index for all other foods for at least the past decade. You may want to try an alternative to brand-name products: store-brand and generic cereals. Generics cost 30 to 40 percent less than name brands, and many taste about the same.

Chocolate Chip Cookies

An excellent cookie must be full of the flavor of browned grain, possibly with hints of butter, vanilla, and brown sugar. Its ingredients should taste fresh. The cookie's surface and edges should be crisp and crunchy; its insides should be moist and chewy.

As for chips, the more chocolaty the better. The makers of some packaged brands suggest they bake as many chips as they physically can into the cookie, as if to turn the confection into a chocolate bar with dough chips. But loading up with chips is no good if the chocolate doesn't measure up. It should be soft, melt smoothly in the mouth, and provide a "hit" of chocolate flavor. Some chips contain cocoa or chocolate liquor, a liquid extract of the cocoa bean, and some have artificial flavor. But a chip's ingredients don't give a clue as to its taste.

Fresh-baked cookies taste best. Among these, two made-from scratch recipes fit the definition of an excellent cookie. The first, a Hillary Rodham Clinton entry in the 1992 *Family Circle* magazine bake-off, won first prize.

Clinton cookies

1½ cups unsifted all-purpose flour
1 teaspoon salt
1 teaspoon baking soda
1 cup solid vegetable shortening
½ cup granulated sugar
1 cup firmly packed light brown sugar
1 teaspoon vanilla extract
2 eggs
2 cups old-fashioned rolled oats
12-ounce package semi-sweet chocolate chips

Preheat oven to 350°F. Combine flour, salt, and baking soda. Beat together shortening, sugars, and vanilla until creamy. Add eggs, beating until light and fluffy. Gradually beat in flour mixture and rolled oats. Stir in chocolate chips. Drop batter in well-rounded teaspoonfuls onto cookie sheets. Bake 8 to 10 minutes or until cookies are done. Cool cookies on sheets for two minutes before placing them on wire racks for further cooling. Yield: 7½ dozen cookies.

Original Toll House cookies

(Ruth Wakefield's recipe with alterations by Consumers Union.)

2¼ cups all-purpose flour
1 teaspoon baking soda
1 teaspoon salt
1 cup (2 sticks) softened butter
¾ cup granulated sugar
¾ cup firmly packed brown sugar
1 teaspoon vanilla extract
2 eggs
12-ounce package (2 cups) Nestlé Semi-Sweet Chocolate Morsels
1 cup chopped nuts (Consumers Union omitted them)

Preheat oven to 375°F. In a small bowl, combine flour, baking soda, and salt. Set aside. In a large mixing bowl, beat butter, sugar, brown sugar, and vanilla extract until creamy. Beat in eggs. Gradually beat in flour mixture. Stir in chocolate morsels and nuts. Drop batter in rounded measuring tablespoonfuls (Consumers Union used rounded teaspoonfuls) onto ungreased cookie sheets. Bake 9 to 11 minutes until edges are golden brown. Yield (using tablespoons of dough): 5 dozen cookies.

Consumers Union's variations

1. *Substitute margarine for butter.* You'll cut saturated fat by two-thirds. The cookie is slightly greasier and has less butter flavor.

2. *Substitute shortening for butter.* You'll cut saturated fat by more than half. The cookie is lighter and puffier, with a delicate crispness. It's also a bit less chewy. Although the butter flavor is gone, the cookie still tastes rich.

3. *Leave out the eggs.* The cookie's cholesterol, low to begin with, becomes even lower. The cookie is very dense, chewy, and greasy, with lots of browned-butter flavor.

4. *Halve the butter; add four tablespoons of water.* You'll halve saturated fat. The cookie is airy but slightly tough and hard, and it loses its browned-butter flavor.

5. *Halve the butter; leave out the eggs; add six tablespoons of water.* Don't bother. You'll halve saturated fat and decrease cholesterol, but the cookie will be tough and hard, and taste a bit of raw flour.

Christmas Trees

When shopping for a tree, grasp a branch about six inches from the end and firmly slide it between your fingers to the tip. If the tree is fresh, no green needles should come off. The tree should also have a strong fragrance and be bright green (or, for blue spruce, gray-green).

Once you get the tree home, saw about an inch off the bottom of the trunk and immediately place the tree in a stand. It's best if the stand holds at least a gallon of water—that's the amount an average tree absorbs in a day.

Clothes Dryers

Dryers vary more in convenience features than they do in performance. Any machine is likely to be able to fully dry just about any washing machine load of laundry. Most midprice dryers have two or three auto-dry cycles controlled by a thermostat, the oldest and most common type of temperature sensor; it senses dryness by measuring the temperature of air leaving the drum. A number of models come with electric contacts that are touched by the clothes as they tumble. This kind of design has the potential to be more accurate because it monitors moisture directly.

One important distinction among dryers—electric or gas—affects the cost of operation. As a rule, gas dryers are much cheaper to run than electrics. At national average utility rates (63 cents per therm of gas and 8.7 cents per kilowatt-hour), it would cost 47 cents to do a 12-pound mixed load in an electric dryer and only about 11 cents in a gas dryer. So, if a gas installation is at all practical in your house, try to take advantage of it.

Venting. To reduce the risk of fire from accumulated lint that gets past the dryer's lint filter and lodges in the venting system, follow manufacturers' venting instructions closely. Avoid flexible plastic duct pipe for venting. It tends to sag, creating obstructions that make it easy for lint to begin accumulating.

The best materials for venting are flexible metal hose or rigid metal, like stovepipe. You can use thin, foil-walled duct pipe, but it tends to deform much more readily than the other metal ducts, allowing lint to accumulate and slowing drying speed.

Coffee, Brewed

After beans are roasted, the freshness clock starts ticking. Vacuum cans, bags with a one-way "freshness" valve—to let gases escape but keep air out—and hermetically sealed bricks are three packaging tricks used to keep beans at their peak. Grinding whole beans just before brewing should make a fresher-tasting pot of coffee—intact beans preserve flavors. Even if you don't go to such trouble, you can improve your chances of getting the freshest possible taste by taking care to store coffee in a sealed, dry, airtight container. Never store opened coffee at room temperature. If you'll finish the coffee within a week, it's all right to keep it in the refrigerator. If you'll have it around longer, put it in the freezer. (You can grind and use frozen coffee without first defrosting it.) And if you buy coffee beans, patronize a store with lots of turnover in the coffee bins.

Coffee Beans

The two most common species of coffee bean are the robusta and the arabica. Robusta beans, mainly from Asia and Africa, make a harsh brew and are used mostly in instant coffee and in cheaper brands of brewed coffee. Arabicas are the beans found in better brewed coffees. Some varieties of arabica are better than others. Brazil arabicas, for example, have an earthy taste and a lower-quality reputation, and so are often blended with higher-quality beans, including Colombian. Arabicas good enough to stand on their own may be sold in single-origin "varietal" coffees—100 percent Colombian, for instance. If no such wording is on a coffee's package, it's probably a blend of several varieties. Ideally, the beans are selected so as to complement one another.

Coffeemakers

Just about all drip coffeemakers can transform water and high-quality grounds into a good cup of coffee. But some are much more convenient to use than others.

Loading. There are three main concerns here: How easily can you fill the water reservoir with the amount of coffee you want? How easily can you fill the brew basket with coffee? And, once fully loaded, how many cups will the machine actually deliver?

Filling the coffeemaker's reservoir with water is easier if it has bold cup numbers on the interior or a marked plastic window or tube that allows you to see the fill level. Most carafes carry cup numbers, too, a nice touch if the reservoir is unmarked. The best are clearly marked on both sides in one-or two-cup increments. Some carafes are marked on only one side, have numbers that are hard to read, or—even worse—have small numbers embossed on their plastic handle. To avoid dribble down the outside of the carafe when pouring, pour slowly, as you would to serve coffee.

The brew basket (which holds the filter and coffee grounds) should be easy to remove and insert but not get in the way otherwise. The handiest baskets have an insert in a frame that swings away from the machine like a door. Some baskets pull out from a slot—not exactly inconvenient, but slightly harder to use than swing-out baskets.

Some coffeemakers have a basket that's dark inside, which shows stains much less readily than the white or light-colored basket found on others.

Capacity. A claim of 10 or 12 cups on the box doesn't mean the same from brand to brand, because manufacturers use different "cup" sizes in their designs. You'll find out quickly enough how much coffee and water you need to use for your requirements.

Brewing. Brewing begins with the flick of the on/off switch. When setting a programmable model, easy-to-use controls are the key. The controls shouldn't be crowded together and they should be easy to read. The on/off light should be easy to find, and the switch should be simple to operate. Since it's easy to leave the coffeemaker on, a prominent on light is important.

Coffee is most pleasing to sip when it's at a temperature of

140°F to 160°F. Since the brew cools in the cup and cools further after you add cold milk or cream, it needs to be hotter than 160°F when brewed and when held in the carafe. Experts say coffee in the pot should be between 170°F and 190°F. Coffee shouldn't be held longer than an hour; some experts say that coffee's flavor begins to deteriorate even 15 minutes after brewing.

The "cup selector" control found on some machines is designed to alter the brewing process when you make only a few cups of coffee. It works well, eliminating the need to add a little more coffee per cup when brewing just a few cups.

Cleanup. Although hand-cleaning carafes, lids, and brew baskets isn't very difficult, the instructions for many machines allow those parts to be cleaned in the dishwasher. Textured housings may look stylish, but they tend to hamper cleaning.

Manufacturers recommend that coffeemakers' innards be regularly descaled, using white vinegar or a descaling solution, to remove minerals deposited by tap water.

The percolator. In a drip coffeemaker, hot water passes through the ground coffee only once, whereas a percolator circulates its brew continually through the grounds. Percolators generally brew more slowly than drip coffeemakers. Many people, particularly those who like their coffee extra strong, prefer percolated coffee.

The French press. This type of coffeemaker consists of a cylinder, usually glass, fitted with a fine metal or cloth screen at the end of a plunger. You put coffee grounds in the cylinder, pour hot water over them, and let the brew steep three to five minutes. Then you push the plunger down, forcing the grounds to the bottom of the cylinder. Brew from French presses usually contains more sediment than drip coffee.

Manual drip coffeemakers. These consist of a glass carafe topped with a filter basket that contains the grounds. You simply pour near-boiling water slowly through the grounds.

Comforters

Comforters are popular, and for good reason. A comforter is more forgiving than a spread if your interest in bedmaking is minimal; and it's at least as warm as a blanket—usually far warmer.

The filling

When you shop you'll see down, synthetic material, and a group of polyesters often called synthetic down. Rare alternatives include silk or cashmere fillings (both very expensive), wool, and cotton (appealing to people who are sensitive to other fills). Each type gives a comforter a different set of attributes. Any comforter placed over a top sheet and a blanket should keep you warm down to about 50°F.

Down. As a rule, down comforters are more expensive than the other common types; thicker than the other types (1½ to 2 inches versus ½ to 1 inch), lighter, and warmer, especially when put inside a fabric cover. Comforters may possibly aggravate allergies.

Comforters labeled "down" must contain at least 80 percent down. The rest can be tufts of torn down and feathers, fibers, even bits of dust. "Feather and down" comforters can be any combination of the two. Fill from a specific bird—as in "goose down"—must contain at least 90 percent plumage from that bird. Some comforters are labeled "white goose down." True, white down won't show through a comforter's white shell, but you'll probably cover the shell anyway.

Down is ideal for keeping you warm, but warmth varies, depending in part on fill power, which is the number of cubic inches an ounce of down occupies if left undisturbed. The higher the fill power number, the plumper and/or lighter the comforter.

Synthetic fill. Eighty-five percent of the comforters sold are filled with polyester fiber. A typical regular synthetic comforter is cheaper than down. It's not as warm as down or synthetic

down but still warm enough for almost anyone. It's thinner than down, as well as being nonallergenic. Synthetic comforters come in a colored cotton/polyester shell that can be somewhat stiff.
Synthetic down. These comforters are priced between regular synthetics and real down. Their warmth is between down and regular synthetic down. They are heavier and thinner than down. They are nonallergenic. These comforters come in a white/beige shell of soft cotton; many people add a cover.

Common Cold

There's no evidence that the common cold occurs because of chilling from inadequate clothing, nor does the chill weaken your body's ability to fight the disease. Colds do occur more frequently in the winter, but that's probably because people tend to cluster together indoors in the winter, making it easier for cold viruses to spread from person to person. The viruses seem to spread readily through skin contact as well as through the air. The best ways to prevent spread are frequent hand washing and keeping your distance.

Computer Buying

With computer prices constantly falling and capabilities rapidly growing, it should be easy to find good values if you're in the market for a computer. But don't expect to have an easy time finding those values in the ads for IBM-compatible computers. Ads for Macintosh computers tend to be more straightforward. These explanations can help you read between the lines:
Monitor. A cheap monitor, although labeled SVGA (shorthand for super video graphics array), may still deliver a mediocre picture. The screen may measure 15 inches, but the viewable area

may be smaller because the case masks part of the tube. Look for a monitor that's noninterlaced, with a dot pitch no greater than 0.28 mm. Also, make sure the video card has at least 1 megabyte of video RAM.

Plug and play. This feature makes it easy to add such components as a CD-ROM drive or a modem. But make sure the machine conforms to Windows 95 standards (look for the Windows 95 logo on the packaging), not the manufacturer's own definition.

Fax/modem. An inexpensive one may pass data slower than 14.4 kbps. Find out before you buy. Have the modem upgraded or choose a different computer. Trial with an online service can be had free from many sources. Membership starts at about $10 to $20 per month.

Processor. An ad that mentions a P-75 processor is ambiguous. It may refer to a 75 MHz Intel Pentium (one of the fastest, most powerful processors) or maybe it's a clone. Some clones don't work as fast as corresponding Intel processors.

Hard drive. A 525MB is the minimum acceptable size on a machine running several applications designed for Windows 95. Eight MB of RAM is just enough memory for Windows 95, which runs better with 12 or 16 MB.

Software. Some computers include an inexpensive Works package and some marginal CD-ROM titles. Dollar values may be inflated by dealer. Software may be older versions.

CD-ROM. Speed should be stated. Look for a quad-speed (4X) drive.

Sound card. Make sure it's compatible with Sound Blaster, the de facto standard for computer audio. Watch out for cheap speakers that don't include an amplifier or A/C adaptor.

Windows, etc. Standard on most computers. Try the mouse and keyboard to be sure they aren't low-quality. Take an older version of Windows only if it comes with a free upgrade to Windows 95.

Computer Printers

Laser and LED page printers create images electronically, using toner, much the same way a photocopier does. They work well with plain, inexpensive copier paper, and they produce water-proof print that won't smudge. This type of printer can do quite well with black-and-white graphics and photos. Ink-jet printers fire ink onto paper from an array of narrow nozzles that form characters or graphics. Despite improvements in technology, text from a good ink-jet printer is still not quite as good as you can get from the best page printers. Graphics are variable in quality. These printers use water-soluble ink that smears easily (use of highlighter can cause smudging). They will accept plain copier paper but may require special coated paper for best results or highest-resolution printing.

Before shopping, ask yourself some basic questions.

Mac or IBM-compatible? Owners of IBM-compatibles enjoy a broader selection of printers. Macintosh owners can choose among Mac-only printers marketed by Apple, which makes Macs, or Mac versions of some IBM-compatible printers. A Mac version usually costs about the same as its IBM-compatible relative.

Printer use. Some low-priced printers are costly to use once you add in the expense of ink or toner. Conversely, some expensive models are quite economical. Cost per page can run from 3 cents to more than twice as much.

What about graphics and photos? Some home computers can even handle snapshots that have been transferred to floppy disk (rather than photo paper) and graphics prepared with kids' pro-grams. A printer that excels at art may cost more than one that excels at text—and a printer that excels at both will cost still more. Therefore, consider how often you'll use photos and graphics, and how good that art will need to look when it's printed out.

Color or black-and-white? In addition to asking how often

you'll print graphics and photos, also ask yourself how often they're likely to be in color. Although the cost of color ink-jet printers has come down, you'll still pay a price for color capability—either in dollars or in compromises in the quality of black-and-white text compared with a similarly priced laser printer. Unless you're sure you need color, choose a black-and white printer.

Combined equipment. If space is tight, a multifunction machine that combines a phone, ink-jet or laser printer, fax machine, photocopier, and sometimes even an image scanner might be appealing. Such a unit can cost much less than buying components separately. But expect some sacrifice in performance and features compared with separate components—and expect different models to be better at different functions.

Condoms

As a means of preventing the transfer of disease-causing microbes between sex partners, condoms have no equal. The need for such protection is apparently greater than many people realize: Every year, 12 million Americans—one-fourth of them teenagers—come down with sexually transmitted diseases. Chlamydia, gonorrhea, and AIDS—as well as other sexually transmitted diseases—are virtually 100 percent preventable with proper condom use.

An estimated 2–5 percent of condoms tear during use. Most of these failures are thought to stem from misuse, not inherent product flaws. (And misuse is common: When the British Consumers' Association asked some 300 Englishmen to demonstrate putting a condom on a model penis, nearly one in five got it wrong—they tried to unroll the condom from the inside out.)

Preventing pregnancy. The condom's reliability in preventing pregnancies depends on how reliability is measured. Researchers don't count the number of individual condoms that fail; instead, they define contraceptive failure as the percentage of women who use a given method but nonetheless become pregnant over a year's time. For condoms, the typical rate is about 12 percent, somewhat worse than birth-control pills but better than the diaphragm. However, researchers know that, as with other methods, the failure figures include many couples who don't use contraceptives every time.

If couples used condoms consistently and correctly, researchers estimate, the condom's pregnancy failure rate would drop to 2 or 3 percent, or perhaps even lower. One way some couples might further reduce the failure rate—to an estimated one-tenth of a percent, if used consistently—is to use condoms in combination with a vaginal spermicide.

Lubrication. Many condoms come coated with various preparations that feel like oil, glycerine, or surgical jelly. Using a lubricated condom is largely a matter of preference. If couples wish to add their own lubricant, they should be certain not to use petroleum- or mineral oil–based products, which rapidly weaken latex.

Cordless Telephones

These telephones are liberating. You walk and talk at will, thanks to an antenna-equipped handset that communicates by radio with the telephone's base. However, the signals from a cordless phone are intercepted much more easily than those on a wired phone line, and it's not uncommon for neighbors to eavesdrop on one another's cordless-phone conversations. Also, static and other noise can hamper the handset's reception as you get farther away from the base.

Many of today's higher-priced, state-of-the-art cordless phones operate on a higher-frequency radio band (900 megahertz, MHz) than older models. The band is less crowded (and so less prone to interference) than the original models. And many phones now use digital transmission. The new technology, while it can make voices sound choppy at long range, does eliminate the snapping, crackling, and popping produced by older, basic cordless phone models. Digital phones are also more difficult to eavesdrop on. The 900 MHz models offer impressive range.

If you own an older cordless phone, you'll probably find a new 10- or 12-channel phone to be noticeably less noisy and longer in range than your present model. Also, it will likely cost less than your old phone.

Credit Cards

What do credit-card offers really mean?

- A low introductory interest rate may be appealing at first glance, but a rate that lasts for at least a year is much better.

- When consolidating debt into a low-rate card, check the offer to find out whether the card company charges you a fee to transfer balances from another company's card to its own. Also, be sure that the balance transfer is not charged as a cash advance. If it is, interest charges may immediately start to accrue at a higher interest rate than you would be charged for purchases.

- Any new card should have a grace period so interest payments won't start to accrue as soon as you make a purchase.

- Cards with no annual fees are quite common. Only about 30 percent of cards carried an annual fee in late 1995.

- Think twice before agreeing to buy credit insurance. It may be free for a few months, but after the introductory period, the monthly premium may be quite high.

- Read the fine print carefully regarding the annual interest rate (APR). It can run to a very high number. Avoid such card offers if you are likely to carry a credit-card balance.

- The line of credit offered in the solicitation to use a card is the top amount possible. It isn't a promise of how much you will actually receive.

Fraud protection. Credit-card fraud is big business, but you can take some precautions to protect yourself. For example, don't give card numbers or expiration dates over the telephone unless you initiated the call. In addition, don't put a credit-card number on a check at a merchant's request; almost half the states prohibit this practice, and Visa and MasterCard won't let merchants bill your credit card to cover a bounced check. If a sales clerk insists, either argue it out with the store manager or walk away from the purchase. Giving in puts far too much personal information— your credit-card number, your checking-account number, your name, and your address—all in one tempting location.

Try not to give out your birth date or your Social Security number more often than is absolutely necessary. Both can be used to apply for a card in your name; if the card is sent to a "new address," you may not know about it until you're dunned for payment. You won't be liable for the charges, but it can take considerable time and effort to clear your credit record. (In states that use Social Security numbers as drivers' license numbers, you may be able to request that a different number be used on your license.)

If a credit card is lost or stolen, your maximum liability is $50—and then only if you fail to notify the credit issuer promptly. So-called card registries, which typically charge about $15 in exchange for a promise to call all your credit grantors in case of loss or theft, are generally not worth joining. Since you'll have to make a list of your cards, their numbers, and their issuers for the registry, why not save the $15 and make the list for yourself? One way to make a list is simply to photocopy all your cards on a sheet of paper and keep it in a safe place.

Tricks and traps. Periodically, your card issuer may alert you to special offers that appear at first glance to be a good deal. Watch out. A common offer, typically surfacing late in the year when holiday bills loom large, lets you skip one month's payment. If you do that, you will pay more in interest overall, and you'll lose out on any interest-free grace period on new purchases, as well.

Your card issuer may also offer to lower the minimum payment it requires from you. This can be a good deal for the card issuer but a costly one for you. If your issuer lowers your minimum monthly payment to, for example, 2 to 3 percent of your balance, that can stretch your payments over many years and triple the interest you owe. Pay each month's balance in full, of course, and you'll avoid interest charges altogether.

Beware of cards bearing "overlimit" fees. These are fees that some banks impose when you go over your credit limit. Among banks that charge them, an overlimit fee of $10 to $15 is about average. And that's on top of the interest you owe on your card's balance.

Cash advances also come at a high cost. Most banks charge interest immediately, with no grace period, along with a fee averaging $2.50. According to one organization, taking a cash advance of $300 with a fee of $2.50 and interest at 18.5 percent from the date of the advance, paid in full the next month, is equivalent to paying interest at an actual annual rate of 32.94 percent on the advance. If you plan to use your credit card to obtain frequent cash advances, look for a card that has a grace period or one that does not charge a fee.

Resist the temptation to accept every new card that comes along. Card users carry an average of between two and three bank cards. That should be more than enough. Each time you apply for a card, that shows up on your credit history. And too much available credit, whether you use it or not, may make it difficult to qualify for a mortgage or other major loan, because potential creditors will fear that you may become overextended.

Cribs and Crib Mattresses

Federal and voluntary standards have eliminated most safety worries. When shopping, base your choice on convenience, price, and looks. Cribs in compliance with voluntary standards usually bear a certification label. But uncertified models often adhere to the rules as well, so don't assume a noncertified crib is less safe than one with a label.

Models with a single dropside are usually cheaper than those with double dropsides. If you plan to locate the crib against a wall, you may want to save money and buy a single dropside. Choose a double dropside if you want access from either side. A double dropside also gives you a backup, should one dropside mechanism break.

Any crib, old or new, should be inspected periodically for wear and tear. Look for broken or missing parts, make sure all hardware is secured, and check for peeling paint. As soon as the child can stand, remove bumper pads, which the child can stand on to climb out.

About hand-me-downs. Cribs made before 1973, when government safety regulations took effect, are likely to pose hazards that have been designed out of new models. But even cribs made just a few years ago can be risky.

Here's what to look for when shopping for a crib:

• Avoid a crib with loose, broken, or missing slats, or slats spaced more than 2⅜ inches apart.

- Make sure the end panels extend below the mattress support at its lowest position, so a child can't get caught in a gap between panel and mattress.

- A lowered dropside should be at least 9 inches above the mattress support at its highest setting, so an infant can't fall out. The top of the raised side should be at least 26 inches above the support at its lowest setting.

- Avoid a crib with a dropside that can be released too easily or that can be opened with only a single motion for each lock.

- Push, pull, and shake the crib by its end panels and sides to gauge the integrity of the hardware and components.

- Be aware of cribs made before 1978, and especially those made before 1970. They may be coated with a finish that contains lead—a toxic hazard to children, who will chew on anything.

Mattresses

When buying, select the firmest mattress you can find, foam or innerspring. Check by squeezing the center and edges. Look for double- or triple-laminated ticking, fabric binding along the seams, and plenty of vent holes.

Carefully measure the crib, especially an older crib, before you shop for a mattress. New crib mattresses must be approximately 51⅝ inches long by 27¼ inches wide. The mattress should fit snugly in the crib. If you can fit two fingers between the mattress and any side of the crib, the mattress is too small or the crib too big, and a child's body or head can get trapped in the gap between mattress and crib.

D

Declaration of Independence

If you have a copy of the Declaration of Independence that has been passed down through the family, you may wonder whether it has any value.

The original declaration, dated July 4, 1776, is on display at the National Archives in Washington, D.C. A number of copies were printed at the time the original was issued. Fewer than two dozen are known to exist, but there may be more. The bottom line of those copies reads "Philadelphia: Printed by John Dunlap." More reproductions were issued in 1818 and 1819 with embellishments that are not on the original. In 1823 there was another printing of several hundred copies, stamped with the name W. J. Stone. Those old copies are valuable, but the thousands made since then have little value. For a list of declaration appraisers, call the Antiquarian Booksellers Association at 212-757-9395.

Dehumidifiers

The basements in many houses are dank. After you have taken care of some basic drying-out steps, among the simplest ways to reduce a basement's moisture level is to run a dehumidifier. The machine works on the same principle as an air conditioner: It wrings moisture from indoors. But instead of pumping the heat and moisture outdoors, a dehumidifier passes the dried air across a set of warm coils and back into the room. The air is drier but also warmer than before.

A large-capacity unit, one rated at or above 50 pints per day, is usually a wiser buy than a small one. As a rule, the larger the capacity, the less time it must run. And while a large dehumidifier can always be throttled back, a small one can't always be turned up enough to bring humidity down as much as you might want.

Before buying a dehumidifier. Before investing in a dehumidifier, it's important to deal with drainage problems: Moisture seepage into a basement is often made worse by landscaping or gutters that allow rainwater to drain toward the foundation. It may be necessary to excavate around the foundation wall. You should also weatherseal doors that lead outside, and keep doors that lead upstairs closed at all times. Close all windows and caulk any cracks around them. Moisture drawn from the surrounding soil can seep through concrete and into the basement. Coat basement walls and floors with masonry sealer.

Be careful not to carry moisture into the basement with items you store there, such as unaged firewood. "Green" logs can give off a surprising amount of humidity.

Dehydration

Don't wait to feel thirsty before you take a drink when you're exercising; by then, your body has started to become dehydrated. That's particularly important for older people, whose sense of thirst is not as reliable as it used to be, and who are more vulnerable to dehydration. To prevent trouble, it's essential to drink water before exercise and water, diluted fruit juice, or sports drinks during exercise. To be safe, avoid drinks with caffeine or alcohol, which are believed to have a dehydrating effect.

Depression/Holiday Blues

Holiday seasons aren't jolly for everyone. "There is no time more socially complex and more psychologically demanding," one psychiatrist has written. "A flood of reminiscences set in a background of enforced joyousness colored with theological and moral hues is ample opportunity for the evocation of negative mood."

The National Mental Health Association offers this advice for anyone hit with a case of the holiday blues:

- Keep your expectations for the holidays reasonable and realistic. Don't strive to make this year's holiday "the best ever."

- Don't try to suppress feelings of sadness or loneliness if they arise.

- Take this year's holiday on its own terms; don't set yourself up for disappointment by trying to make it just like the good old days. Try something new.

- Minimize your drinking. Excessive alcohol consumption will only make you feel more depressed.

In some cases, what appears to be the holiday blues might actually be a bout of clinical depression. The typical symptoms of depression include not only a persistent sad or empty mood but also fatigue and decreased energy; feelings of guilt, worthlessness, or helplessness; and often, thoughts of death or suicide.

The National Institute of Mental Health conducts a program to encourage early identification and treatment for people who suffer from depression. For a free brochure, call 800-421-4211.

Dips and Chips

Everyone knows that reaching for a vegetable platter is healthier than reaching for a bowl of potato chips. But once you start using the broccoli to scoop up sour cream onion dip, the tables are turned: Dipped vegetables give you about 60 percent more fat and calories than potato chips straight from the bag. And dipping in fat-free honey dijon dressing isn't necessarily a more prudent choice. Fat-free dressing can have the same number of calories and twice the sodium of full-fat dip.

Dishwasher Detergents

Most people choose powdered dishwasher detergents, either regular or the ultraconcentrated variety. Liquid gels are easier to pour into the machine, but some may not wash as well as many powders.

Over time, a harsh detergent may damage glassware, fine china, sterling silver, and silver plate. In hard water most products aren't likely to damage glasses. Damage to glasses is apt to be greater in soft water because ingredients in the products meant to "neutralize" the minerals in hard water instead attack glass, at first turning the glass iridescent, or producing a frosty haze that over time would turn opaque. As for sterling silver and silver plate, it's safest to wash these items by hand. Use the smallest amount of detergent that will give you clean dishes.

Dishwashers

Within the mid-price range of $300 to $500, dishwashers do a very good job of getting dishes clean, despite their increased energy efficiency.

Spending more will buy more features, not cleaner dishes, since brandmates usually have similar washing systems. Expensive models often have electronic controls, which are somewhat easier to use than push buttons and dials. Some have better insulation to suppress noise.

There are top-of-the-line dishwashers that offer "fuzzy logic" technology, which chooses the number and length of washes and rinses on the basis of the amount of soil in the wash water. Although these machines wash well and offer appealing convenience features, they may not save water or perform better for you than a regular machine, and they are expensive—costing as much as $600 to $700 or more.

Narrowing down the choices. Beyond good washing, quiet operation, and energy efficiency, you may want to keep other things in mind when you select a dishwasher:

- Additional wash cycles for items like pots or fine china usually add to the price. Three settings are all you need—a light cycle for less-soiled loads; a normal one for a typically soiled load; and a heavy cycle for hardened soils. Most people stick with the normal setting. Pots, fine china, crystal, and silver are best washed by hand.

- Fold-down trays let you fit more cups on the upper rack.

- A terraced upper rack lets you load tall items upstairs on one side and gives clearance for large items on the other side below.

- A covered basket is useful for holding small items in place.

- Adjustable tines can be angled so you can load larger items.

- An upper rack that adjusts for height is important if the machine has a center spray arm, which can limit height in both racks.

- If your dishes are larger than 10 inches or have a cupped edge, bring a few along when shopping to check for fit.

Portable dishwashers. Portable machines, for kitchens without the space for a built-in dishwasher, are just like built-ins except that they come in a cabinet on rollers and hook up to the faucet for use; they can be converted to built-ins later.

Doctors

A *Consumer Reports* survey of more than 70,000 subscribers revealed some potentially serious problems with the doctor-patient relationship.

A significant number of respondents reported that their doctors weren't open to questions and didn't discuss the side effects of drugs they prescribed.

The most dissatisfied patients were not those with the most serious diseases but rather those with chronic, bothersome, and difficult-to-treat ailments, such as back pain and headache. Helping those patients may require more discussion and support.

People whose doctors didn't communicate well with them were less likely to follow their doctors' instructions.

Men scored male and female doctors about equally, but women found female doctors were better than male doctors in terms of caring, communication, and thoroughness.

Door Locks

Whereas burglars may disarm locks with sophisticated methods such as picking, many break-ins through a door involve physical attack on the door and lock. A door lock and door plate are no stronger than the door and jamb in which they're mounted. Therefore, it's premature to think about upgrading the door locks in your home until you consider the security of the doors themselves. The best doors are made of metal-clad or solid hardwood, hung in metal or hardwood framing. The doors should fit closely and swing smoothly on strong hinges.

Here are four ways to lock a door:

• *Entry lockset.* The primary lock found on most exterior doors, it is a short, spring-loaded latch released by the lock's knob or handle and locked by a key on the outside knob or a button or lever on the inside knob. Guarding that main latch is a secondary latch that makes it impossible to push back the main latch with, say, a credit card forced between the door and the doorjamb.

- *Entrance handleset.* This has a latch, which doesn't lock, worked by a thumb lever, and an auxiliary key-operated cylinder deadbolt lock. A long, decorative handle is mounted below the thumb lever. .

- *Surface-mounted deadbolt lock.* From outside the home, this is unobtrusive, mounting flush with the door. On the inside, however, it protrudes from the door. Some models have two vertical bolts; others have horizontal bolts.

- *Cylinder deadbolt lock.* The key and thumbturn at opposite ends of the cylinder control a deadbolt that extends an inch or so into the door. Unlike the spring-loaded latches on primary locks, deadbolts don't automatically engage when the door is closed; they must be locked manually. Double-cylinder deadbolt locks have a keyed cylinder on the inside of the door as well as on the outside.

If the primary locks on your doors are entry locksets, and they're working fine, there's probably little to gain by replacing them. If you want to make your doors more secure, start by beefing up the hardware in their doorjambs. Install a high-security strike plate, one with heavy-gauge metal and screws 3 inches long.

Good auxiliary locks are far from invulnerable. However, when equipped with the right hardware, they will protect your home from all but the most determined burglars. The cylinder deadbolt is the least obtrusive auxiliary-lock design.

A single-cylinder model, with an easily operated thumbturn on the inside, allows a fast, safe getaway in an emergency. If you have glass in or around a door, you may want a double-cylinder lock that has a key, rather than a thumbturn, on the inside.

If you can tolerate their ungainly appearance, surface-mounted deadbolt locks offer good protection against burglars who might try to kick or jimmy their way into your home. Surface-mounted locks are generally easier to install than locks that must be inserted into the door.

Drain Cleaning

You may be able to avoid having to use caustic, dangerous chemicals for opening clogged drains if you take a few preventive measures. For example, avoid pouring grease down the kitchen sink. Whenever possible, do not pass kitchen waste through the garbage disposer either. Trash or compost it instead.

In addition, be sure sinks, tubs, and showers have strainers to trap food, hair, and the like. Clean the strainers regularly, and periodically remove and clean the drain-plug mechanism in bathroom sinks and tubs. That mechanism is a common place for hair that's escaped the strainer to lodge and form an obstruction. (The hair, in turn, can become a filter for soap, skin oils, and other residues carried by the water.)

Pouring hot water into a drain is unlikely to clear a clog, but a weekly dose of boiling water can effectively keep a drain running freely. Heat about a gallon of water, pour in half, wait a few minutes, and then pour in the rest. Be careful to pour the water directly down the drain, not on the basin or tub, and never use this technique on a toilet bowl. Boiling water could crack the porcelain.

Another way to avoid having to use dangerous drain-opening chemicals is to keep a couple of mechanical drain openers around the house. A snake is the most versatile device, since it can both break up a greasy clog and snag clumps of hair. Unlike a pressure device such as a plunger, the snake can remove all or part of a blockage, limiting the chance that the clog will be liberated only to flow down the drain and cause trouble elsewhere.

Economic Statistics

Here's a quick guide to some of the most influential economic statistics issued by the U.S. government and what they can mean to you:

Consumer Price Index (CPI). This is a measure of the average change in prices paid by urban consumers for a "market basket" of goods and services, including food, clothing, shelter, transportation, and prescription drugs. The items in the index are averaged and given weights that relate to their importance in overall spending.

The overall CPI probably won't match your own budget. If you have hospital bills or college tuition to pay, your spending for those items will be far higher than what the CPI considers average for a household. For that reason, the CPI is often faulted as an unrealistic measure. Nevertheless, the CPI remains influential. For one thing, it's used by employers in calculating salaries and pensions, and by the government in determining cost-of-living increases for Social Security recipients.

Producer Price Index (PPI). This index provides a clue to the future costs that consumers will pay. When producers receive higher prices from retailers for their products, it's likely that those increases will be passed on to consumers. A major increase in the PPI may be a signal to stock up on nonperishables or to consider buying a car this year instead of next.

Unemployment rate. In the simplest terms, this is the number of unemployed people divided by the number in the total labor force, expressed as a percentage.

However, the government counts people as being employed even if they worked only one hour in the surveyed week, and it doesn't include as members of the labor force so-called discouraged workers—people who might be able to work but who haven't actively looked for a job in the preceding four weeks.

Gross Domestic Product (GDP). This is a measure of the total value of all finished goods and services produced within the United States. GDP eliminates production abroad but includes production in the United States by foreign-owned companies. A rising GDP points to a strong and expanding economy; a falling GDP is associated with higher unemployment and overall economic weakness.

Index of Leading Economic Indicators. This number includes initial claims for unemployment insurance, new orders placed to manufacturers, residential building permits, money supply, and the length of the average work week. The index is considered a predictor of what will be happening to the economy six to nine months in the future and is worth looking at before you make any major career or financial moves.

A strong dollar (or a weak one). The strength of the dollar translates in practical terms into its value when compared with other countries' currencies. When the dollar is strong, it is worth more yen, francs, lire, pounds, and so forth. For American consumers, a strong dollar means that you may be able to buy imported goods for less money than would otherwise be the case. It also means that your money is worth more when you travel abroad.

A weak dollar isn't necessarily bad news. It means that the United States is a better deal for tourists from other countries; it also can be a boon for U.S. manufacturers because the exchange rate may make their goods cheaper for foreigners and therefore easier to sell overseas.

Eggs

If you're already eating an egg every day and your blood cholesterol is moderate, you can relax; your body's cholesterol regulator clearly is working properly. Go ahead and enjoy eggs. They're an inexpensive source of high-quality protein and are fairly low in saturated fat. One egg contains about as much fat as you'll find in an 8-ounce glass of 1 percent milk. And eggs are an important staple for the elderly.

Grades. The "grade" designation on the carton doesn't refer to size or nutritional quality but rather to the structure of the yolk and whites. The higher-grade AA eggs have thicker whites and firmer yolks than grade A eggs of equal freshness, so they spread out less in a pan. AA eggs cost a bit more but make shapelier poached and fried eggs. They also age a little more gracefully, if it takes you some time to use up a dozen eggs.

Once you bring eggs home, don't bother to transfer them to the egg rack on the refrigerator door. The eggs actually keep best in their carton on a middle refrigerator shelf. The carton shields eggs fairly tightly, and the shelf is apt to be cooler than the egg rack.

Germs. Bacteria can enter an egg through the pores in the shell, and even "good" eggs can occasionally cause illness. Fortunately, cooking eggs thoroughly kills the bacteria. Here's what to do to be especially prudent:

- Avoid raw or undercooked eggs—runny omelets, sunny-side-up, uncooked hollandaise and bearnaise sauces, and homemade foods that use raw or partially cooked eggs as a recipe component. And avoid nibbling uncooked cookie dough or licking cake batter from spoons or other implements.

- Cook egg dishes thoroughly, and consume them promptly—or refrigerate them. Do not keep eggs warm for more than an hour.

- Keep unused eggs at 40°F or cooler, and discard any with broken shells.

- Wash your hands and cooking utensils with soap and hot water immediately after touching raw eggs, to avoid contaminating other food.

Electric Blankets and Mattress Pads

Fewer people buy electric blankets than buy comforters, and fewer people still buy electric mattress pads. But blankets and pads have their attractions. They warm up the bed before you climb in and keep it warm even if you get up in the middle of the night.

Electric blankets and mattress pads come with a number of warnings: Don't use more than one electric blanket or pad on the bed at the same time, use the bedding on the bed size it's designed for, don't tuck cords under the mattress, and don't cover a warm electric blanket with any covering more substantial than a thin blanket or lightweight spread.

Electric bedding is safer than it was a few years ago. Back then, blankets and pads emitted very high electromagnetic fields (EMFs), which some studies have linked to potential health problems. The current crop of blankets and pads have far lower EMFs—close to the "background" level produced by any house's wiring. Nevertheless, it's prudent for pregnant women to use an electric blanket or pad only to warm the bed before climbing in, to avoid the risk of overheating the fetus.

Electric blankets have evenly spaced wires everywhere except their edges, to heat evenly. Pads, on the other hand, have more wiring at the bottom than at the top, an arrangement that reflects the body's tendency to lose heat faster from the feet and legs than from the upper body.

Some blankets have a feature that is claimed to send extra

heat to cold parts of the body. These "smart" blankets seem to work as advertised, but so do some blankets and pads that don't make any such claims.

Top-of-the-line blankets are usually woven of 100 percent acrylic fabric. This makes for an especially soft blanket. Lower-priced blankets are often 20 percent acrylic and 80 percent polyester, which adds strength. Mattress pads are generally 100 percent polyester.

Twin-size blankets and pads come with one control box; full-size, with one or two; and queen and king size, with two. All controls are likely to work well.

Electric Ranges

Decades of competition and technological tinkering have made the conventional electric range—the kind with coil elements—inexpensive and dependable. Almost any model should be able to cook at least competently.

The newer smoothtop range performs no better than a conventional model. Its cooktop, made from impact-resistant ceramic glass, looks sleek. But a smoothtop range is more expensive than the conventional variety, is slower to heat, and for best results requires flat-bottomed pots and pans that should be close to the same size as the burner. Although not difficult to clean, a smoothtop requires a special cleaner.

A conventional range heats food fast, is forgiving of pots and pans with warped bottoms, and has elements that are easy to replace. If space is at a premium, a conventional range's surface can't be used as a countertop, but a smoothtop's can (with the burners off).

Controls. On almost all ranges, dials control the cooktop burners. A smoothtop range usually has a digital clock/oven timer, set by keypad, and an additional keypad for controlling oven temperature. The typical conventional range still keeps time with an analog clock and controls oven temperature by dial. However, it's becoming more common for a conventional range to have a digital clock/timer, sometimes combined with a keypad for controlling oven temperature.

Dials and mechanical clocks may be an advantage to a range when it comes to reliability. Ranges with keypads have been a little more trouble-prone than those with control dials.

What about gas?

Many people like cooking with gas because it's instant-on, instant-off. Gas burners can accommodate pots without flat bottoms, such as woks. Energy costs for gas versus electricity favor gas for cooking, and a gas cooktop can be used in a power outage. However, gas ranges are more expensive to buy than electrics and are more likely to need repair.

Energy Conservation

Air leaks in the home can push utility bills as much as 40 percent higher than they need be. Caulk, insulate, and seal cracks, crevices, and ducts. In cold regions, storm, double-pane, and "low-emissivity" windows (which use a film coating to reduce heat loss by preventing reflected long-wave infrared radiation from escaping back through the glass) are a good choice if you are remodeling. Look for wood or vinyl window frames—or aluminum with a nonconducting layer, called a thermal break (regular aluminum frames conduct heat so well that they could cancel your energy savings). Draperies can also help retain a home's heat.

Turning a thermostat down from 72°F to 68°F in winter can save about $80 a year. Most convenient is a thermostat that lowers the temperature automatically at times you've set on it.

Central heating. If your furnace hasn't had any attention in the last few years, you might realize a 10 percent boost in efficiency—and money saved. The local utility or service company can calculate efficiency by analyzing your furnace's exhaust gases. At $50–$100, such a checkup might be well worth its cost. In a forced-air heating system, change the air filter at least once a year.

Water heating. A hot water heater set at 140°F is wasting energy and money. Insulating the heater may help. A $20 insulation kit can save as much as 20 therms a year on heating bills ($12 at average gas rates) or 700 kilowatt-hours of electricity ($58). Another option: Set the heater to 120°F, which can save up to 10 percent in water-heating costs.

Air-conditioning. Buy an energy-efficient (high EER) unit of the right capacity for your space. (Shades help cut cooling costs, too). If your area isn't very humid, you may find that a whole-house fan or ceiling fans provide adequate comfort, and for a lot less money than air-conditioning.

Trees. Planting one or more trees gives summertime shade and increases property value.

Appliances. Government programs and innovative design have made today's appliances far more energy-efficient than their predecessors. Replacing a 15-year-old refrigerator with a new, high-efficiency model can cut the refrigerator's energy cost by $70 a year.

Effective refrigeration. A good energy-saving temperature is 37°F to 42°F in the refrigerator, 0°F to 5°F in the freezer (any warmer, and food will spoil too easily). Check temperatures with a refrigerator-freezer thermometer. Make sure the door gaskets are clean and tight enough to grip a sheet of paper. Replace the gaskets when necessary. At least once a year, clean the condenser coils under or behind the unit. Dusty coils make a refrigerator (or freezer) work extra hard.

Washing temperature. Up to 90 percent of the energy consumed by a washing machine goes to heating water, says the

Association of Home Appliance Manufacturers. Reserve hot water for heavily soiled loads. Switching the wash-cycle water to warm will cut energy consumption in half. Always rinse with cold water—it won't affect how clean the clothes come out.

Drying clothes. Plan your washes with drying in mind: Separate lightweight items, which need less drying, from heavy ones. Try to dry full loads, and don't overdry. Clean the lint screen frequently, so warm air can flow freely.

Lighting. About a sixth of the electricity used in a home goes into lighting, and much of it is wasted. About 90 percent of a typical incandescent bulb's electricity is lost as heat. According to one estimate (not including the cost of new fixtures, where required), replacing a typical home's three most-used incandescent bulbs with compact fluorescents and the rest with tungsten-halogen lamps would save $30 a year in electricity costs. It would also mean changing bulbs less often: Higher-efficiency bulbs tend to have longer lives. Energy "miser" bulbs are not a very good idea. They save 5 to 10 percent in power but deliver 5 to 10 percent less light.

Make sure bulbs are clean—dust can cut light output by perhaps 10 percent. Install dimmers to reduce light when it's not needed. And turn off any light you're not using—turning a bulb back on doesn't require extra energy.

The automobile. Keeping a car's engine tuned can save 3–8 percent in gasoline. A clogged air filter alone can cut fuel economy by one mile per gallon. Underinflated tires can also reduce fuel economy: They increase the car's rolling resistance.

Higher speeds demand more fuel. Driving at 65 miles per hour instead of 55 drops fuel economy 15 to 20 percent (smaller cars suffer most). Most cars attain their highest fuel economy at 45 miles per hour. Try to drive at a steady speed. Jackrabbit starts and repeated acceleration and braking waste gas.

If you must sit in the car for more than a minute or two, turn off the ignition. An idling engine consumes up to a gallon of gasoline an hour.

Exercise During the Day

People involved in exercise regimens may wonder what time of day is best for obtaining the greatest benefits. They may have heard about medical studies suggesting that morning exercise increases the risk of heart attack, or that strength and flexibility peak in the afternoon. But you can't rely much on the results of such studies because they were small and often so were the differences they found. In fact, it seems that any time of day should be fine for a workout.

You'll get the most benefit when you find a convenient time that enables you to stick with a routine. However, right after a heavy meal, light exercise such as walking is fine, but a vigorous workout should be put off for an hour or so, After you eat, your body sends extra blood to the digestive organs, leaving less available for the heart and muscles.

Exercise During Winter

When you exercise outdoors in cold weather, you collect a bonus, since the body burns extra calories just staying warm. However, the danger of hypothermia requires an extra degree of caution when walking, running, skating, and skiing. This life-threatening danger can occur even at outdoor temperatures well above freezing, especially if you're wet and tired. By the time symptoms occur—including slurred speech, blurred vision, loss of coordination, and confusion—the body has lost its ability to generate heat. At the first hint of such symptoms, it's essential to get out of the cold immediately, put on warm, dry clothing, and seek medical help. The Penn State Center for Sports Medicine suggests these precautions to avoid hypothermia:

- *Bring a buddy.* At the least, let someone know your route and when you expect to be back.

- *Dress smart.* Avoid excessive sweat accumulation by wearing removable layers of loose clothing. An outer nylon shell deflects wind.

- *Warm up well.* Allow more time than usual, wear heavier warm-up clothing, or warm up indoors.

- *Consider the wind.* Start out facing into the wind so you'll confront the harshest conditions while you're fresh.

- *Drink up.* Cold weather may diminish your thirst but not your need for fluid—vital for generating body heat.

- *Keep going.* Sustained exertion generates heat; stopping to rest loses it.

Exercise Machines

Working out on a home exercise machine—a scaled-down version of a fancy health club model—offers certain advantages. It's more convenient than going to a club, generally safer and more comfortable than exercising outdoors, and usually gentler on the joints than working out on hard floors or pavement. Unfortunately, many people eventually find that they don't really like the machine they've bought. To find out whether an exercise machine is likely to hold your interest, suit your fitness level, not aggravate any joint problems, and be easy enough to learn, you need to give it a thorough tryout—at least 5 to 10 minutes, preferably more—at a health club, a friend's home, or a store. The machine you choose should feel sturdy, move smoothly, be reasonably quiet, and let you mount and dismount easily. And it should fit your body comfortably, without cramping your movements or forcing you to lean, stoop, or stretch.

Find out whether the store will assemble the machine for you. If not, ask to see the instructions; assembly may be too complicated and time-consuming for you. Note that some products' makers offer toll-free technical support.

Treadmills

A treadmill is essentially a wide belt stretched over a bed between two sets of rollers. The most common type is motor-driven.

Advantages. Walking or running on a motorized treadmill is a fairly natural, enjoyable exercise as machine exercise goes. Most treadmill beds have some give to them, making the workout easier on the joints than walking or running on hard pavement. Increasing the incline lets you walk uphill, which can provide as strenuous a workout as jogging with far less pounding.

Disadvantages. Motorized treadmills are typically noisier, more expensive, and more likely to break down than other machines.

What to look for. The treadmill belt should be long and wide enough to accommodate your stride, and the motor should be powerful enough to move the belt without any pauses or jerks. More expensive machines have the desirable characteristic of letting you start the machine gradually rather than immediately starting you out at the speed used at the end of your last exercise session.

For safety, beginners should look for a machine with long handrails on each side of the belt, and everyone should look for one with wide footrails. Choose a machine with an emergency button that stops the treadmill immediately. On some models, a tether running from your clothing to the console stops the machine automatically if you fall.

Ski machines

A cross-country ski machine lets you exercise using movements similar to the scissoring stride and rhythmic pole-pushing of real cross-country skiing, an activity that burns more calories per minute than almost any other aerobic exercise. Unlike running, walking, stair-climbing, and bicycling, cross-country skiing works both the upper and lower body. Because it involves most major muscle groups, it requires more energy than localized workouts like weight lifting. It doesn't subject the joints to jarring impact, as running and high-impact aerobics do, so the risk of injury is relatively low. And it's strenuous enough to permit exercise for long periods of time, providing the kind of workout that benefits the cardiovascular system.

There are two major types of machine: those with independent leg motion (the skis can slide back and forth independently of each other) and those models with dependent leg motion (the skis are linked by a belt or chain, so that when one goes forward, the other goes backward).

Independent machines are more difficult for a novice to master but are more enjoyable to use once you get the hang of them. (Typically, they're also more expensive.) The performance differences stem from the dependents' linked-leg design. Although that design helps keep a beginner's legs from sliding too far, it also forces them into an unnaturally stiff shuffle.

A dependent machine is worth a look if your level of fitness is fairly low or if you find it tough to get the hang of independent leg motion.

Stationary bicycles

The pedals on stationary bikes turn a large flywheel, fan, or both. On flywheel models, you can increase resistance without changing speed. On fan-only models, the only way to intensify the workout is to pedal faster, which boosts air resistance to the fan. Bikes with a fan, unlike those with just a flywheel, generally have movable handlebars that work the upper-body muscles.

Advantages. Stationary cycling requires minimal learning, balance, or coordination. On models with motionless handlebars, you can read while exercising. And indoor bikes are less likely to break down than other aerobic machines.

Disadvantages. Stationary cycling uses fewer muscles than the other machine workouts do, and it's not as good for the bones as the other workouts, since the skeleton doesn't have to bear much weight body weight in the sitting position.

What to look for. A comfortable, properly adjusted seat is crucial for safe, enjoyable use. If you don't like the seat during a store tryout, try to get the management to exchange it for one that's more comfortable. Make sure you can adjust the height so your leg extends almost completely when the pedal is all the way down. To avoid knee strain, check the alignment, too: With the ball of the foot on the pedal spindle and the pedal in the three o'clock position, the top of the shin should lie directly over the spindle. If not, see whether the seat can be moved forward or backward. The handlebars should be adjustable, too; some models let you shift to the "drop-bar" position used by road cyclists.

Another important feature to look for is a flywheel or fan that doesn't stop turning the moment you stop pedaling the bicycle. (Otherwise, you have to strain to get the wheel or fan moving again after each pause in your pedaling.) Get a machine with pedal straps, which allow the legs to work on the upstroke, making the exercise more vigorous and working the hamstring muscles at the back of the thigh, and counterweights, which keep the pedals upright, making it easier to slip your foot into the straps. Avoid exposed spokes or holes in the flywheel, which can amputate a finger.

Stair climbers

All stair climbers basically consist of two pedals that alternately drop under your weight to simulate climbing up stairs or rungs. On one type of stair climber, called a stepper, the handles move back and forth if they move at all. The other type, called a ladder, always has movable handles, which you move up and down from a point above your shoulders or head.

Advantages. Both types of stair climber cause little jarring, so they're fairly easy on the joints, although they aren't recommended for people with knee problems.

Disadvantages. The pedals may rise and fall either dependently—pushing one pedal down jacks the other one up—or independently. Even at the lowest resistance, some independent stair climbers may be too hard for people who are out of shape, older, or overweight.

What to look for. Make sure the machine can't be readily tipped over if you lean too far in any direction.

On steppers, check the angle of the pedals during the upstroke. They usually slant downhill as the pedal arm rises: Some slant enough to make the feet slide forward, jamming the toes against the front of the shoe. (The pedals on better steppers and on most ladders typically remain parallel to the floor.)

The difference between dependent motion and independent motion is less important for stair climbers than for ski machines, but climbers with independent motion can provide a more vigorous workout.

Extended Warranties

It's easy to see why retailers push extended warranties (or service contracts) so hard. Stores can make more money by selling extended warranties, which can cost hundreds of dollars, than they can from the sale of the merchandise. One trade group asserted: "No other product on your sales floor offers so much profit potential."

It's estimated that fewer than 20 percent of products covered by an extended warranty are ever brought in for repair, either because they don't break during the warranty period or their owners prefer to replace them when they do. It's wise to avoid purchasing extended warranties.

Eyesight Damage

Reading in dim light or using cheap, off-the-rack reading glasses can't damage vision. Reading in dim light is no more injurious to the eyes than straining to hear a whisper is to the ears. Store-bought reading glasses are perfectly safe and work fine for most people with presbyopia (farsightedness due to aging eyes). The fact is, poor lighting and the wrong lenses—whether off-the-rack or prescription—can cause eyestrain, but they won't harm your eyesight.

Wearing "extended-wear" contact lenses overnight, on the other hand, does threaten eyesight. Even a single night increases the risk of a potentially blinding corneal infection. Closely following the manufacturers' sterilizing regimen doesn't eliminate that risk.

F

Fast Food

Most fast-food restaurants offer salads or grilled-chicken sandwiches, some of which are good in both taste and nutrition, especially if you omit their dressing. But you can make even a "regular" fast-food meal more nutritious by following a few rules:

- *Hold the mayo.* While you're at it, hold the tartar sauce and other mayonnaise-based dressings on sandwiches and salads. Order the sandwich plain, or scrape the mayonnaise off.

- *Omit the cheese.* One slice adds about 3 grams of fat and 40 calories to a sandwich. A hamburger made with two slices of Swiss cheese, plus mayonnaise and bacon, has the fat of about five regular hamburgers. Holding the additions spares you more than 240 calories and 22 grams of fat. Skip only the cheese and mayo, and you could still substitute a medium order of fries for the fat you save.

- *Dip with discrimination.* As if chicken nuggets didn't have enough fat, fast-food chains serve them with sauce. At least one had 17 grams of fat per serving. However, some dips have little or no fat, but they do add calories.

- *Skin the chicken.* If you cut straight to the meat, you could lose about a third of the calories and half to three-quarters of the fat. Skinless fried chicken is much healthier, too.

- *Develop a taste for baked potatoes.* A serving of french fries generally has more fat and calories than a small hamburger does.

A baked potato has no fat at all when eaten plain. A pat of butter adds 4 grams of fat and about 30 calories.

Fat-Free Foods

If your first priority is cutting fat, eating fat-free foods will help. But so will low-fat foods, or a dietary plan that helps you eat less of everything overall. The choice is one of personal preference. (Cost need not be an issue. It is generally possible to pay about the same for fat-free and regular foods.) If you choose no-fat foods as a quick route to cutting calories, however, don't expect your palate to be pleased.

If you're looking for a happy medium—reduced calories and fat but pretty good flavor—consider low-fat varieties. At 50 and 60 calories per two-tablespoon serving, for example, a low-fat salad dressing is a reasonable substitute for a full-fat one. And a low-fat mayonnaise will fill in for full-fat mayo, especially when it's mixed with other foods. You might also consider training yourself to eat smaller—or fewer—portions of full-fat foods. Use 1 tablespoon of full-fat salad dressing instead of 2.

One word of caution: If your goal is to lose weight, don't use the no-fat label as a license to eat more. Whether you're eating no-fat, low-fat, or full-fat products, more food inevitably means more calories. And adding calories—with or without fat—will eventually add pounds.

Fats in the Diet

Tropical oils (coconut oil, for example) and animal fats (including butter) are especially high in saturated fat. Safflower, sunflower, and corn oil are high in polyunsaturated fat; olive and canola oil are high in monounsaturated fat. Trans-fatty acids are present in margarine, in such processed foods as cookies and crackers, and in such restaurant foods as french fried potatoes.

Different fats affect blood cholesterol in different ways:

- *Saturated fat.* As a rule, if you increase your intake of saturated fat, you'll raise your blood-cholesterol level; if you decrease your intake, you'll lower it.

- *Polyunsaturated fat.* When people substitute polyunsaturates for saturates, their total blood-cholesterol generally drops.

- *Monounsaturated fat.* Olive oil is very high in monounsaturated fat, the kind that lowers low-density lipoprotein (LDL) in the blood. LDL is often called the "bad" form of cholesterol. LDL deposits cholesterol on the inner lining of the coronary arteries, where it can accumulate and block blood flow. High-density lipoprotein (HDL)—"good" cholesterol—protects the arteries by transporting cholesterol to the liver for disposal.

Whereas foods rich in polyunsaturates lower both forms of cholesterol, dietary monounsaturates lower LDL and often leave HDL alone—a better combination. That may explain the low rate of coronary artery disease among Greeks and southern Italians, who have a high-fat diet but get much of that fat from olive oil.

Fax Machines

Whereas the typical fax message still travels from one corporate office to another, the shrinking price and size of a basic fax machine has made faxing practical for the home office, too.

Since you probably would not want the expense of a separate

phone line for a fax machine, those intended for home use typically have circuitry that monitors incoming calls, routing voices to the phone and fax tones to the machine. Virtually every fax machine for the home can also double as a basic photocopier.

Expensive office machines print on plain paper. Relatively inexpensive machines for the home use thermal paper, which has its drawbacks. The print on thermal paper tends to fade over time when exposed to light, and because thermal paper comes in rolls that fit into the machine, fax printouts must be cut into pages, which tend to curl. However, spend a little more and you can get two useful features: an automatic paper cutter and a document feeder.

On some machines with a cutter, as the fax paper is fed from the roll, the cut pages tend to curl. Printouts are easiest to handle when machines cut paper and then flatten it with an anti-curling system that "irons" the pages.

More features

Easy dialing. Home models offer at least a few one-touch dialing buttons that you can program for frequently called numbers. More numbers yet can be programmed through speed-dialing—you press a special dialing key, then one or two digits to make the call.

Auto retry. When your fax machine reaches a busy signal, most will automatically redial persistently for at least a few minutes until a connection is made.

Memory, broadcasting. If some models run out of paper when receiving, they can capture a few pages of text in memory for printing later. This feature, found on more expensive home machines, also makes "broadcasting" possible—you can store a document in the memory, then send it on to a roster of phone numbers. Storage capacity depends on how dense the text is (fewer single-spaced pages can be accommodated than double-spaced pages, for example).

Delayed sending. This feature lets you set up a document to transmit at a later time, often up to 24 hours later, to take advantage of cheaper phone rates. Your originals must be loaded into the document feeder or the machine's memory, if it has one.

Polling. Normally, the fax machine that places the call also sends the document. Polling, found on most fax machines, permits the opposite. The receiving machine can dial up, or "poll" another fax machine to retrieve a document from it. The fax machine supplying the document must be set up and waiting. Polling is the fax version of calling collect: Someone can pull a document from your fax machine without your incurring the cost of the call.

Activity reports. At the touch of a button or two, most faxes print various reports—a listing of documents recently sent or received, for example, with phone numbers, times and dates, and the success of each transmission. Such reports can be useful for record-keeping. Some fax machines can also print a summary of their electronic settings, a directory of the numbers programmed into memory, and other electronic options that are in effect.

Fiber in the Diet

There is a substantial body of research showing that fiber can lower cholesterol levels, protect the heart, and probably reduce the risk of cancer.

Manufacturers' claims can now tell you at a glance whether a food supplies a significant amount of fiber:

- Products with the words "good source of fiber" or "contains fiber" must provide 2.5 to 4.9 grams of fiber per serving.

- Foods labeled "high" or "rich" in fiber must provide at least 5 grams.

- Products making a health claim about coronary disease or blood-cholesterol levels must contain lots of soluble fiber— more than 6 grams.

If a package of bread—or cereal—carries none of the FDA-approved claims that would identify it as a significant source of fiber, look for any of these reassurances on the label:

- The words "whole wheat" or "100 percent whole grain."

- Whole-wheat flour listed as the first ingredient. (If it's listed lower down, the bread contains less than 50 percent whole wheat, usually much less.)

- At least 2 grams of fiber in each slice of bread or each one-ounce serving of cereal.

Getting more fiber. Eating at least five servings per day of fruits or vegetables and at least six servings of whole grains or beans— the amounts recommended by the U.S. government—generally ensures an ample intake of fiber.

Here are several ways to boost your intake of those high-fiber foods:

- Bake with whole-grain flour instead of refined flour. Choose brown rice over white rice, and whole-wheat pasta over regular or even spinach pasta.

- Substitute whole, unpeeled fruits for fruit juices.

- Add fruit, brown rice, or whole-grain cereals to yogurt.

- Add beans, barley, or other whole grains to soups. Snack on cooked, cooled beans seasoned with garlic powder, chili powder, or Cajun spice, or make them into a bean dip for raw vegetables.

- Prepare cold salads that combine cooked whole grains, pasta, or beans with chopped raw vegetables. (Don't depend on lettuce-based salads for fiber. Even the otherwise nutritious loose-leaf types of lettuce contain less fiber per serving than white bread does.)

- Make meatless entrees by cooking grains in seasoned stock and tossing them with cooked vegetables or beans.

Film

As film ages, it loses contrast and its colors shift. But exceeding a roll's expiration date by a few months shouldn't affect the quality of photos much, provided the film has been stored in a cool place (the refrigerator or freezer is ideal). Images generally deteriorate after exposure, though, so try to finish a roll quickly and develop it right away.

Speed

The "speed" of a film refers to its sensitivity to light. The least sensitive, or "slowest," film demands more light than faster stock but is otherwise superior. Each doubling of film speed—from a sensitivity rating of ISO 100 to ISO 200, say—halves the amount of light needed but slightly reduces the color accuracy and increases the graininess of the printed image.

Print films may be as slow as ISO 25 or as fast as ISO 3200. As a rule, the faster a film's speed, the higher its price. The fastest films can capture sharp, if grainier, images by candlelight without the use of a flash or a tripod, But most amateur photographers stay with film rated at ISO 100, 200, or 400. At those speeds, differences in the quality of 4 x 6-inch prints are quite subtle. But the slower the speed the better, if you expect to make 8 x 10 or 11 x 14 prints.

Color-print film is more forgiving than it used to be, especially to overexposure. With the greater latitude of today's films, you can make all but the worst overexposure errors and still have pictures turn out fine. (Of course, most cameras now select the ISO setting, exposure, and aperture automatically, eliminating grievous errors of judgment.) Wide film latitude allows simple cameras that lack an ISO 200 setting to expose 200 film at an ISO 100 setting; the processing lab can usually be depended on to automatically make the small adjustment needed to produce satisfactory prints. However, the machines aren't infallible, and neither are the humans whose job it is to check their work. If prints disappoint you, return the negatives and ask that they be reprinted. Reputable processors don't charge for such reprints.

Fire Extinguishers

A fire is an unpredictable event that can turn within seconds from a gentle smoldering to a wall of smoke and flame that defies a household extinguisher. You should err on the side of caution when deciding whether to tackle a blaze. If the fire is rapidly growing, if it is very smoky, or if there seems to be a risk that flames might spread to block your exit, leave the job to professional firefighters.

If you do choose to fight the fire, don't begin your work until you've called the fire department and you are sure everyone else is out of the house.

Types of fires

Fire extinguishers are grouped by the kinds of fire they're meant to fight. Fires are classified as "A," "B," or "C," according to the type of materials burning.

"A" fires. Fires of ordinary combustibles—paper, wood, cloth,

upholstery. "A" fires are the only kind you can safely and effectively extinguish with water.

"B" fires. These involve flammable liquids—cooking grease, gasoline, paint solvent, fuel oil. One of the most common "B" fires is a grease fire in the kitchen. Unlike most other fires, grease fires are often contained and so can often be extinguished by smothering. For a stovetop fire, turn off the heat under the pan and cover it with something fire-resistant—a lid or baking pan. To smother a fire in an oven or broiler, try turning off the heat and closing the oven door. If the blaze doesn't quickly subside from lack of air, use a dry-chemical extinguisher on it. Never try to move a blazing pan or pour water on any grease fire—that can spread the flames by spattering the burning liquid.

"C" fires. These involve electrical equipment—TV sets, receivers, fuse boxes, wiring, and the like.

Types of extinguishers

Companies sell multipurpose A:B:C extinguishers for home use. They can smother most kinds of fire. There are also B:C models that fight only fires involving flammable liquids and electrical equipment. Experts say that in a pinch you can use a B:C extinguisher on an A-type blaze—a burning wastebasket, for instance. Although the extinguisher may not put out the fire, it may at least slow the flames. (You should not have to walk more than 40 feet to an extinguisher, nor should you have to reach too high, across obstacles, or into places that are ablaze.)

The designations for fire extinguishers applied by Underwriters Laboratories (UL), an independent safety organization, include numbers in front of the As and Bs that denote the sizes of fire of those types that the unit can quell. The result is a UL rating such as 2-A:10-B:C or 5-B:C (no sizes are assigned to "C" fires, the electrical variety). If all other factors are equal, an extinguisher that's rated at, say 10-B should be able to handle as much flaming liquid as a 5-B unit can extinguish.

Your extinguishers should be in good working order. Check their pressure at least once a month. Extinguishers with a dial-type pressure gauge are easy to check—a needle shows at a glance whether the unit has sufficient working pressure or is undercharged. Smaller models often omit the dial in favor of a pressure check pin on the nozzle assembly: You push down on the pin; if it pops back, the pressure is all right. Be sure to look at the pressure before you buy an extinguisher, too.

Most extinguishers can be recharged after a fire or if their pressure drops over time. Recharging an extinguisher is less wasteful than throwing it away. However, a recharge may cost nearly as much as a new extinguisher and may not provide the same firefighting characteristics as the original factory charge. Models not built to be recharged should be replaced after about 12 years, or sooner if the manufacturer's instructions recommend it or if the extinguisher's pressure has ebbed.

Choosing an extinguisher

Your first choice should generally be "ful-floor" models—those large enough and versatile enough to cover an entire level of your home against fires of all common burning materials. Choose a full-floor extinguisher rated at 2-A:10-B:C only if its slightly shorter height and lighter weight, compared with a larger model, is important to you. Otherwise, a 3-A:40-B:C model is the wiser choice.

Additional coverage for individual rooms is available from supplemental models. A 1-A:10-B:C unit would be a good choice for a den. A small B:C extinguisher is worth considering for the kitchen, where its sodium bicarbonate spray will be more effective on a grease fire than the spray from a multipurpose extinguisher.

Safety check. Familiarize yourself with the basic steps to operate an extinguisher:

1. Pull the ring pin or, on some models, break a paper seal: Stand the recommended distance from the fire (look at the extinguisher's label) and aim low and toward the fire's base, along its front edge and sides.

2. Squeeze the handle or, on some models, press the button.

3. Sweep the spray from side to side, as though you were hosing down a sidewalk.

If the fire doesn't shrink quickly, get out without delay.

Fish

Follow these guidelines to be sure the fish you buy is both fresh and wholesome (federal rules don't guarantee that fish will be uniformly clean and high-quality):

- Use your nose. Fresh fish smell like the sea, but without a strong odor. Freshwater fish often smell like cucumbers. Strong odors usually indicate spoilage.

- When buying whole fish, look for bright, clear, bulging eyes. The gills should be bright red and moist. Cloudy, sunken, discolored, or slimy eyes often signal fish about to spoil. Whole fish should be displayed on ice, away from hot lights.

- When buying steaks or fillets, look for moist flesh that still has a translucent sheen. If the flesh is dried out or if the fibers are beginning to pull apart, the fish is old. Fillets displayed in separate pans surrounded by ice indicate that the retailer is mindful of quality.

- Be wary of cooked seafood displayed next to raw fish. That represents a potential health hazard.

- Refrigerate the fish you buy quickly. Keep it in its original wrapper, in the coldest part of the refrigerator, and use it within a day.

- Clean cooking surfaces after you've used them to prepare the fish, to avoid spreading bacteria.

- Cook the fish thoroughly. It should be opaque and flake easily with a fork.

Food Labeling

In addition to requiring the nutritional information on the back or side of a package, the U.S. Food and Drug Administration (FDA) has established rules for certain claims and adjectives that appear on the front of a package. Manufacturers used to be free to use terms like "light" or "healthy" at their own discretion. Now these and other nutrition terms have been strictly defined. Manufacturers must meet the standards or take the words off their products.

Some of the terms have now been defined using "daily reference values"—figures based on government recommendations for the consumption of fat, saturated fat, cholesterol, sodium, vitamins, and fiber. For example:

Low, as in low fat, has various specific definitions. For instance, a low-fat product has three grams of fat or less per serving; a low-saturated-fat product has one gram or less per serving and gets no more than 15 percent of its calories from saturated fat; a low-calorie product has 40 calories or less; and so on.

High, as in high fiber, is for foods that contain 20 percent or more of the daily value for that nutrient per serving. A high-fiber food, therefore, has at least five grams of fiber per serving.

Light means a food has half the fat or one-third the calories of its regular counterpart.

Reduced, as in reduced sodium, means a food has at least 25 percent less of the substance named (or 25 percent fewer calories) than a regular product.

Free, as in sugar-free, applies to foods that have none of the substances cited, or a nutritionally insignificant amount. A product may be sugar-free, for instance, if it has less than one-half gram of sugar per serving and fat-free if it has less than one-half gram of fat per serving.

Serving size is no longer up to the manufacturer but is determined by the FDA for 139 product categories and is based on surveys of what people actually eat.

Calories per serving are followed by the number of calories from fat.

Total fat is listed in grams and in the context of a 2,000-calorie-a-day diet. If you consume more or fewer calories, you'll need to adjust the figures accordingly.

Saturated fat is listed separately because studies have linked a high intake of saturated fat to heart disease. Look for low numbers under % Daily Value for saturated fat, cholesterol, and sodium.

Total carbohydrate includes *dietary fiber,* which belongs in a prudent diet. The FDA doesn't recommend a specific daily limit for *sugars,* also listed with carbohydrates, but they basically provide calories without nutrients.

No reference value is listed for *protein.* The government recommends that most people on a 2,000-calorie diet eat about 50 grams a day (a small hamburger has about 12 grams), but eating enough protein isn't a worry; most Americans get plenty of it.

Food Mixers

If you often make bread and cookies from scratch, a stand mixer is useful and convenient. It can handle heavy baking chores that a hand mixer can't.

Heavy duty. These models offer the most power and the largest mixing bowls. Leading brands have a stationary bowl and a single flat beater that orbits the inside of the bowl as it spins. These mixers also come with a dough hook and a whisk. They can handle at least six cups of flour, enough for two loaves of bread. On most models, the beater head can be tipped up so you can remove the bowl. With the heaviest units, the head stays put; the bowl moves up and down with a crank.

Medium duty. These differ from the heavy-duty type in that they can handle less bread dough—3½ cups of flour at the most —enough for one loaf of bread. They're also lighter, less powerful, and cheaper. These mixers come with one large and one small bowl and a pair of beaters. One beater has a curved bottom and rides against the inside of the bowl to rotate it. They also come with dough hooks.

Light duty. These are essentially hand mixers resting on a stand. In fact, you can even detach them and use them as hand mixers.

Hand mixers. A good one is relatively inexpensive and may be all you need for mashed potatoes, cake batter, whipped cream, and other moderate and light chores.

Multipurpose food fixers. These machines combine stand mixer, blender, food processor, and salad maker. Despite their versatility, it's probably a better idea to buy a stand mixer if that's the appliance you want and need. If you need a food processor or blender, it's wiser to buy them separately rather than buy a jack-of-all-trades appliance.

Food Wraps and Containers

A good food wrap or container should keep foods' moisture and odor in as well as keep outside moisture and odors out.

Aluminum foil. Sturdy and versatile, molds tightly to a drumstick or to tent a turkey. An effective barrier to moisture and odors, but relatively expensive and easily punctured. Comes in three thicknesses: regular, about 0.6 mil thick (1 mil is a thousandth of an inch); heavy duty, 0.9 mil; extra heavy, 1.5 mil. The thicker the foil, the more puncture-resistant. Aluminum foil is better than plastic at keeping oxygen from food and, consequently, helps prevent meat from tasting rancid.

Plastic wrap. These wraps are easy to use because the plastic clings to itself and lets you see what you've wrapped. The best wrap is clear and made of polyvinylidene chloride. Others are made of polyethylene or polyvinyl chloride (PVC). Most PVC wraps are less effective at moisture and odor retention; polyethylene wraps are less effective at odor retention. Both are less puncture-resistant.

Because of the tendency of a wrap's chemicals to migrate into hot food, and because some foods should be covered when they're microwaved, it's prudent to leave an inch between food and wrap when microwaving. Be sure, too, to turn up a corner of the film (or poke holes in it) to help vent steam.

Even these procedures won't help if you're microwaving very fatty or sugary foods, which can generate temperatures high enough to melt many wraps and make them sag. It's probably best to use a plastic-wrap covering only when microwaving dishes like vegetables or dry food.

Paper wraps. Freezer paper, plastic-coated on the side that touches the food, is strong, wide, moisture-resistant, and easy to write on. But its overall effectiveness is not as good as aluminum foil. For example, it won't stay folded unless taped in place. Waxed paper is all right for short-term storage, but it is weaker than freezer wrap. It is best used to keep hamburger patties or cheese slices separate or to wrap sticky foods.

Cellulose bags, made from highly purified wood pulp, are expensive and shouldn't be used with very moist foods because cellulose absorbs water.

Food bags and freezer bags. The typical food-storage bag is three times as thick as plastic wrap, and freezer bags are thicker still. The added thickness tends to make freezer bags more resistant to punctures than are food bags. Frozen freezer bags, however, can be damaged if they're dropped: If one falls as you're taking it out of the freezer, check for holes. Zippered bags are a little handier to use than the twist-tie type.

Plastic containers. These offer excellent protection from moisture and very good protection from unwanted odors. Reusable containers have a few drawbacks: Plastic can retain odors from stored foods and so must be cleaned thoroughly. Oily residues can be hard to get rid of. And stored food can suffer from freezer burn or turn rancid if the sealed container holds too much air.

Fragrances

It's easy to buy a gift of fragrance for someone whose taste you know. You can buy a duplicate of what he or she already wears. Or you can try a fragrance similar to one you know he or she likes. It's harder when you don't know the person's taste, or when you know she or he likes to try various scents. You have to shop around, just as you do when scouting out a new fragrance for yourself.

But shopping in the usual way can steer you wrong. It's quite useless to sniff the testers displayed on department-store counters, or to spray the air around you. With fragrances, first impressions are often misleading.

The blends that perfume chemists put together are designed to create different impressions (known as notes) at different times. The *top notes* are the scents you notice right after you open the fragrance and for the first 10 or 15 minutes or so that the perfume is on your skin. Then the *middle notes* surface.

These are the scents that dominate for the next several hours. That's why, when you sample fragrance testers in department stores or drugstores, knowledgeable sellers will suggest that you apply the fragrance to your skin and wait several minutes before taking a whiff. Ideally, you should wait at least 15 minutes (and purists suggest going outdoors) so that when you do sniff, you sample the long-lasting middle notes. The *end notes* are the scents that serve as the basis for the fragrance; they last until there's nothing left to smell. The ideal fragrance is one that ages gracefully, pleasing the wearer when it's first applied and continuing to please until it's no longer detectable.

Applying a fragrance to your wrist is pointless if you're buying a gift for someone else. The bottled chemicals react with the skin's chemicals, so the same fragrance can smell slightly different from one wearer to another. Instead, spray the fragrances on unscented tissues (don't forget to label the tissues). Sample a few fragrances, allowing them to breathe for 15 minutes or so. At that point the middle notes will have surfaced and you can sniff the tissues.

Remember, a perfume doesn't always have a stronger scent than the same scent in cologne form.

Furnace Efficiency

If the furnace in your house is more than 20 years old, chances are it wastes more than one-third of the fuel it burns. New furnaces are much more efficient and therefore cheaper to run. Some convert practically all of their fuel into usable heat. But that doesn't necessarily mean the most efficient furnace makes economic sense.

Unless your fuel bills are especially high, it probably isn't worth replacing an old furnace if it still performs satisfactorily. If you haven't done so in the past couple of years, have the furnace tuned up so it runs as efficiently as possible. As part of the tune-up, consider these improvements:

- Replace the fuel nozzle on an oil-fired furnace with a smaller one, a procedure known as derating. It makes the furnace run for longer periods but consume less fuel overall. Derating works best on older furnaces that aren't sensitive to such changes in the combustion system.

- Replace the pilot light on a gas furnace with an electronic ignition system.

- Have the duct system checked for leaks, and insulate any exposed ducts that run through unheated spaces. Have a gas furnace's heat exchanger examined periodically for leakage of dangerous combustion gas. If you have hot-water heating, remove any trapped air.

Replacing a furnace

If you decide to replace an old furnace, you need to decide whether it will pay to buy the most efficient unit you can find. Even a new run-of-the mill furnace will be more efficient than its predecessors from the 1960s or 1970s. All new residential-size furnaces are required by federal law to carry an Annual Fuel Utilization Efficiency rating, or AFUE, and to achieve an AFUE of at least 78 percent. By contrast, a gas furnace from the 1960s or 1970s probably has an AFUE of 65 percent; an oil-fired furnace of the same vintage would have a slightly higher AFUE. New furnaces with an AFUE up to 85 percent are often called mid-efficiency. Typically, furnaces that condense some of the water in the flue gas and have an AFUE of 90 percent or more are called high-efficiency.

You want to be sure that you can save enough fuel within a reasonable time to cover the higher cost of a high-efficiency furnace. The fuel saving, however, depends largely on the old furnace's efficiency, not just on the new one's.

The price of furnace efficiency

If you are replacing a 20-year old furnace—one with an AFUE rating of about 60 percent—the following table can help you decide between a new mid-efficiency furnace and a new high-efficiency one. The figures assume that the high-efficiency furnace would cost about $1,300 more than the mid-efficiency one. The far-right column indicates the number of years it would take to recoup the difference in cost between the mid-efficiency and the high-efficiency model.

FURNACE COSTS

Current annual heating bill	Saving 80% AFUE	Added saving 95% AFUE	Years to payback
$ 600	$150	$ 71	18
800	200	95	14
1,000	250	118	11
1,200	300	142	9

Choosing a company to install a new furnace

Begin with the company that services your existing furnace, or with the local utility company (it may provide you with names). If you're not happy with the company with which you now do business, ask for names from friends or neighbors.

Treat the installation of a new furnace as you would any other expensive home-improvement project: Solicit bids from more than one company; ask the companies for references and check them; steer clear of contractors who offer you a price without coming to the house to look at the work involved.

Tell the contractors whether any rooms are too hot or too

cold in the winter; changes to the ducts or piping may be needed to balance the temperature in individual rooms. Contractors should inspect the ducts or piping for proper size.

Don't assume that you should buy a furnace with the same heating capacity as the one you are replacing; many older furnaces have more capacity than they need to provide adequate heat to a drafty or poorly insulated house. If you add insulation or build an addition, you'll probably need a furnace with a different heating capacity.

Connecting a new furnace to the rest of the heating system can be simple or complicated, depending on the amount of space in the furnace room and the difference in size and design between the old furnace and the new one.

The most effective protection against faulty installation is contractual. The agreement should specify that you will make the final payment to the contractor only after the furnace is installed and you're sure that it runs properly.

If you decide on a high-efficiency furnace, there's a chance that it will require more frequent repair than other furnaces because of its greater complexity. It's prudent to buy a maintenance contract from the installer to cover cleaning, checkups, and labor charges for warranty work for at least the first five years.

Garage Door Openers

Garage door openers sometimes operate relentlessly. Since 1982, openers have included a mechanism that automatically reverses the door within two seconds of striking anything in its path. Still, according to the U.S. Consumer Product Safety Commission (CPSC), more than 50 children have been killed in the ten years prior to 1994 because they were trapped and crushed by a moving garage door. To further reduce the risk of injury or death, Congress directed the CPSC to issue a rule requiring openers made after January 1, 1993, to have more than just autoreverse. There must be a provision for the door to reverse on contact. You should check a door opener's autoreverse feature regularly. Lay a 2 x 4 flat on the garage floor where the door touches the ground. Use the opener to close the door. When the door edge contacts the board, the door should reverse within two seconds. If it doesn't, adjust the opener's sensitivity or hire someone to do that.

Every opener comes with at least one remote control, a radio transmitter about the size of a cigarette pack, that can be encoded to open only your door. Also standard is a wall switch that operates the opener from inside the garage.

Openers are built for use with a properly balanced garage door in good repair—not a warped door, or a door that binds in its tracks, has broken springs, is hard to budge off the ground, or doesn't stay put when you hoist it about waist high by hand. An unbalanced door also closes with excessive force.

Convenience features

Remote control. Most openers provide for more than 1,000 different code settings, which should deter any intruder. For safety reasons, opener manufacturers caution against opening or closing the garage door unless it's in plain sight.

Disconnect. A rope-and-latch disconnect permits disengaging the trolley from the door with a pull on the rope—a necessity in the event of a power failure, say. Most openers have a "lock-off" feature that lets you work the door by hand after you've disconnected the trolley, without holding on to the disconnect rope. All openers let you relatch the trolley by hand, which you'd need to do if a power failure occurred when the door was closing.

Lights. An opener's head has at least one socket for a lightbulb; it's usually covered with a diffuser. The bulb automatically lights up as the door opens or closes. The bulb stays lit for at least four minutes once the door is completely shut.

Many wall controls include a "vacation" switch that makes the opener ignore all radio signals. That could be useful when you go on a trip.

Lost the remote? Three types of controls, sold as optional accessories for most openers, can come to the rescue. An electronic touchpad provides better security against break-ins than key-operated devices.

Installation. A do-it-yourself installation requires respectable mechanical skills and about a full day's work. With openers sold at stores such as many discounters and home centers, you have to fit together and assemble sections of rail, connect the rail to the power head, then mount the whole thing on the ceiling and connect the opener to the door. Finally, you have to install the electric eye that senses the door's descent and activates the autoreverse mechanism, and make adjustments that limit the door's travel and reverse force. The job can take six to eight hours.

Openers sold by garage door specialists require less assembly time, largely because their rails come fully assembled. Offsetting that advantage is the possible disadvantage of transport; it's not easy to carry a 9- to 11-foot-long track in a compact car. Such models may have incomplete or hard-to-follow instructions, and they may also lack hardware to hang the power head. If you hire someone to handle the installation, figure on spending around $100. But if you buy an opener from a garage door installer, the premium can be quite high.

Garbage Bags

Garbage bags are marketed under different names—trash, rubbish, scrap, wastebasket, kitchen, lawn and leaf—and on variations of those themes—tall kitchen, large kitchen, and large trash and lawn bags. That makes it easy to pick out the wrong size. What's more, bag size may vary considerably within those groups. As a result, matching the bag to the trash container can be tricky. Here's a brief guide to bag sizes:

GARBAGE BAG SIZES	
Type of bag	*Usual capacity*
Waste	4–8 gal.
Tall kitchen	13
Trash	30–33
Lawn and leaf	39

Any kitchen bag should mate easily with almost any standard kitchen wastebasket. Best are those with a star-shaped seam at their base instead of the usual horizontal seam. They sit flush against the bottom of the wastebasket.

Most trash bags claim to fit inside 30-gallon garbage cans. In reality, many fit but barely, and not without a struggle. Such problems exist because garbage-can capacity is measured in different ways—when filled to the brim or with the lid on, for instance. And cans rated at the same capacity come in different heights, widths, and shapes. As long as no industry standard exists, some bags won't fit some cans.

Thickness. Common sense suggests that thicker is better, but that's not always true. The type of plastic, the quality and amount of recycled material, and the manufacturing process also come into play. Kitchen bags measuring ½ mil thick (a mil is a thousandth of an inch) are sometimes tougher than bags twice as thick.

Material. Most garbage bags are made from one of three polyethylene resins. Some brands specify their type of plastic; with others you can often tell by feeling the bag.

Bags made of low-density polyethylene are soft and pliable. Those made of linear low-density polyethylene are stretchier still. Their main asset is resistance to tearing. Bags made of high-density polyethylene (HDPE) are stiffer and more translucent than the others, and they crunch like tissue paper when touched. Because the material is inherently tough and resists punctures, HDPE bags can be made thinner than others without compromising strength. One drawback with HDPE: A little nick easily turns into a big rip.

Garbage Disposers

A garbage disposer is installed under the kitchen sink and attached to the drain opening and the plumbing. Water and waste flow into a grinding chamber, where metal impellers mounted on a motor-driven turntable grate food against a stationary metal ring. The finer the grind of food particles, the more easily they'll be carried through drains and the less likelihood of a clog. The ground particles are washed out of the disposer and down the drain by a constantly flowing stream of water from the kitchen faucet. The ground-up scraps flow directly from your sink to a sewage-treatment plant or septic system, where they break down more rapidly than they would in any landfill. More than 90 municipalities (including Denver, Detroit, and Indianapolis) consider home garbage disposal so effective in reducing the dumping and incineration of waste that a disposer is required in all new-home kitchens.

Such regulations mark a reversal from the days when major cities banned disposers out of fear that their use would lead to water shortages and an overstrained sewage system. Most of the bans have been rescinded.

A garbage disposer rarely uses more than a very small proportion of a household's water. Disposers can grind most loads of waste within seconds. Using a disposer for a minute consumes about as much water as a fairly efficient toilet uses in a single flush, and half or less of what most dishwashers require for a typical cycle.

Special considerations come into play when installing a disposer in a home where waste does not drain into a municipal treatment system. Disposers are not recommended for cesspools and may even strain a septic system that's already operating close to its capacity. Before buying a disposer, those with septic systems should call their local public health office and find out the recommended system size for use with a disposer. Expanding the size of a septic system is often prohibitively expensive.

Types

There are two type of disposer, continuous-feed and batch-feed. With a batch-feed disposer, you load the chamber and push down or twist a stopper to begin grinding. Continuous-feed machines are activated before loading, using a switch that's usually mounted on a wall close to the sink.

A continuous-feed disposer is more convenient, especially if you generate lots of waste. With a batch-feed machine and too much garbage for one load, you have to fill the disposer's chamber, place the stopper in the drain, wait while it grinds, and then repeat the process.

Batch-feed models are the least prone to hazards, since it's impossible to turn one on unless the stopper is in, covering the drain. That makes them a better bet for households with young children.

All disposers need fast-flowing water to carry waste through them and through the drain under the sink. Manufacturers recommend you turn on the faucet before activating the machine and allow water to run a short while after grinding is complete to flush all waste down the drain. Cold water is recommended because it solidifies grease so it's more easily carried away.

Disposers emit noise mostly through the sink opening. A batch-feed machine's sink stopper also acts as a muffler, making those disposers a little quieter. But no disposer is quiet. Before they're even "fed" food, they make a low vibrating hum. The noise increases a little when soft food is added, and reaches a loud rattle when harder materials such as bone are processed.

Jams. In case of a jam, a built-in overload switch protects the electric motor by shutting it off. Clearing a jam—*always with the power turned off with the manual wall switch*—requires rotating the turntable to loosen the lodged waste. Some models provide a wrench designed to turn the disposer's driveshaft manually. The tool fits into an opening on the bottom of a disposer and can loosen most jams with a single turn. If the impediment won't budge (or no wrench is provided), you can usually dislodge the fragment by poking a broom handle down the sink and into the disposer, using the broom as a lever to rotate the turntable—*always with the power turned off.*

No-nos. Manufacturers have a long list of things not to put down a disposer—leather, cloth, string, rubber, seafood shells, artichoke leaves, corn husks, glass, china, metal—either because those items can damage the machine or because they can be dangerous projectiles if they are ejected. If one of these things accidentally slips into the machine, turn it off and re-

move it (or the pieces) with a suitable implement or hand tool.
Installation. Batch-feed disposers are usually more expensive to buy. But since they don't require a separate electrical on-off switch, they may be less costly to install.

Unless you're replacing a disposer (and can use existing electrical and plumbing connections), figure on the expense of an electrician and perhaps a plumber. The former will be needed to install the switch (on continuous-feed models) and probably to "hard-wire" the appliance into a regular 15- or 20-amp circuit (outlets are seldom found under a sink). Even if you've installed electrical wiring on other projects, you should probably call an electrician rather than tinker with a disposer's combination of electricity and plumbing.

Splashing. A disposer sometimes backs up and floods the sink, creating a mess. But only continuous-feed models splash water and eject food into the sink during disposal. The fixed or removable rubber splashguards that fit into the sink opening may help to minimize the problem. Batch-feed models don't eject food, since the drain is covered during disposal.

Gas Ranges

About half the people who go shopping for a range have no option other than to buy an electric range—their house has no gas hookup. Those who buy a gas range do so because they like the gas range's instant response, its visible, controllable flame, and its baking ability.

Today's gas range is better than the gas range of old. For example:

The oven. It's larger than it used to be.

Broiling. Unlike older gas ranges, many of today's models have a broiling burner at the top of the oven, just like electrics. That leaves the bottom drawer for storing baking pans and the like.

Self-cleaning. Widely available on gas ranges now. It adds $100 or so to a range's price, but it's a lot more convenient than doing the job yourself. And cleaning an oven's accumulated spills with its own heat—upward of 800°F—is cheaper than using an aerosol cleaner. The process works well enough, by and large, on both kinds of range, although the outside surfaces may become very hot.

Controls. Many gas models have electronic touchpads and buttons for setting baking and roasting time, oven temperature, and oven function. The gadgetry adds convenience: Just as a digital stereo tuner locks precisely on a desired radio frequency, electronic time and temperature controls let you be precise about oven settings. Of course, electronic controls add to a range's price. They also add to the possibility that the model will someday need repairs.

Note that the electronic controls are only for the oven. The cooktop burners still have dial controls. With the dials, you turn to the "start" point, at which a clicking electronic igniter lights the flame, then turn to the desired flame intensity. People who are accustomed to older gas ranges may find this a bit disconcerting at first. But at least the worrisome days when the pilot light occasionally went out are over.

Cooktop cleaning. Some models have sealed burners, which keep spills from leaking down under the cooktop. Standard burners on other models lift out easily, exposing an under-cooktop area that's a lot less cluttered than in the old days and therefore a lot easier to sponge off.

Cooktop speed. Most gas ranges are still slower than electrics; they take an extra ten minutes or more to boil water for a big batch of pasta, for example. Some models with high-speed burners are still slower than the electrics.

Low-heat cooking. Smaller, lower-heat burners are relatively new; they're promoted as being helpful for simmering soup or cooking delicate sauces. They generally work quite well, but many larger burners can cook just as slowly.

Types

Most gas ranges sold are 30 inches wide, freestanding, with four burners and a single oven. However, a 30-inch freestanding range is not the only choice.

Gas ranges come in widths from 20 to 36 inches. Some models have a second oven—which can be conventional, convection, or microwave—on top of or beside the main oven.

You can also choose the modular, built-in approach, building a separate gas cooktop into a counter, say, and mounting a gas or electric wall oven somewhere else.

You can even go for a commercial-style range, complete with high-output burners, expansive oven, and a long list of options. These big ranges are for people who consider themselves *serious* cooks.

Glue

The material to be bonded isn't all that matters in selecting a glue. Sometimes the choice is simple. Sometimes it's complicated by the job at hand—its size, the surfaces to be joined (whether they are clean or ragged, for example), and whether water resistance is important.

To check a hard plastic's suitability for gluing, apply adhesive tape to it; if the tape doesn't stick, neither will most glues.

Here's a basic guide: For *hard plastic*, first try plastic cement or superglue. Then consider a urethane, epoxy, or acrylic cement. For *wood*, an emulsion wood glue is best, but for outdoor work, use a resin glue. *Metal* is best repaired with superglue for small jobs; epoxy for large jobs. Try superglue gel for small jobs involving *ceramic*, epoxy for large jobs. Then consider plastic cement. For a *glass* item, especially if it will be washed, use epoxy cement. A second choice would be superglue. Use gel if the break is ragged, liquid if the break is smooth.

Halogen Lamps

Most manufacturers of halogen lamps made for home use enclose the filament in a heat-resistant material, usually quartz, and put the bulb inside a second glass shell. That shell blocks ultraviolet radiation, which can cause skin cancer, and offers protection from the heat that halogen lamps can produce. If a desk lamp, which may be positioned close to a skin surface, has a "bulb within a bulb," it should be safe to use.

Hands, Smelly

Try removing hand odors, onion or garlic residue for example, by rubbing them on a stainless steel sink or a piece of stainless steel flatware with cool water running. You might also try a paste made of baking soda and water.

Hazardous Waste at Home

It has been estimated that the average American household discards about 20 pounds of hazardous waste each year. A product or substance is considered hazardous if it's flammable, explosive when exposed to heat or sudden shock, corrosive or caustic to living tissues, toxic, or radioactive.

Most hazardous household products fall into one of four

broad categories: automotive products (brake fluid, antifreeze, used oil), household cleaners (oven cleaners, bleaches, disinfectants, drain cleaners), paints and solvents, and pesticides.

If you use up the product, you generally need only throw the container in the trash. (In most communities, you can't recycle any container that has held hazardous materials. Rinse out household-cleaner containers before discarding them.)

When some of the product remains, the product and container require proper storage and disposal. That's true whether the rest of your garbage is put in a landfill, burned, composted, or recycled.

For options in your area, contact your local environmental or public-health agency.

What not to do

A few hazardous materials such as laundry bleach and some household cleaners, which are normally fed into the sewer system, can be safely flushed down a toilet or drain. But don't do this with other wastes because a sewage treatment plant can't break down all toxic substances. Don't pour them down a storm drain, either. From there, they're likely to go to a sewage treatment plant or directly to waterways.

Don't dump them in a ditch or backyard. They can poison local plants and wildlife, contaminate soil where children play, and leach through soil to ground water.

Don't throw them out with the trash. They can injure sanitation workers and damage equipment. Chemicals can react with other substances in household trash, leading to a fire or explosion in trucks or waste-handling facilities. In a landfill, chemicals can form a poisonous brew that may find its way into ground water. If incinerated, they can contribute to air pollution.

What to do

Buy just the amount you need, and use it up. If you can't use it up, see whether someone else can. Friends, neighbors, or housing rehabilitation programs may be able to use leftover paint, for example.

Take them to a household hazardous waste day. Your local sanitation authority should know whether your town sponsors a collection day and which wastes are accepted.

Store them carefully. If you must store hazardous materials in anticipation of a collection day, keep them in well-ventilated racks, out of reach of children and animals. Store them in the original container, sealed tightly and kept dry.

Heartburn

The main symptom of heartburn is a burning sensation behind the breastbone after a heavy or spicy meal. The discomfort is caused by stomach acid backing up into the sensitive tissues of the esophagus.

For years, the over-the-counter mainstays for relieving heartburn have been antacids, compounds that reduce the acidity of gastric juices to a more comfortable level.

Competition arrived in the summer of 1995, with a new family of over-the-counter heartburn treatments, the H2 blockers. They work by reducing the production of gastric acid, not just by neutralizing it. These compounds have been in use for a long time but were available only as prescription drugs. The new formulations use the same active ingredients as the prescription drugs but in smaller doses. The first brands to appear were famotidine (Pepcid AC) and cimetidine (Tagamet HB).

Avoiding heartburn. Of course, if you live right, you may be able to eliminate heartburn without drugs. Here's how:

Avoid or cut back on the foods that can trigger heartburn—alcohol, chocolate, peppermint and spearmint, and fatty foods. Those foods tend to relax the sphincter at the entrance to the stomach. Alcohol also stimulates acid production. Smoking, being overweight, taking nonsteroidal anti-inflammatory drugs (such as aspirin or ibuprofen), can make the problem worse.

Since caffeine boosts gastric acid, too, avoid caffeine-containing substances, including coffee, strong tea, soda pop, and various over-the counter medications (read the labels).

Let gravity work for you. Don't lie down with a full stomach. (Better to take a walk instead.)

If you suffer from heartburn at night, elevate the head of your bed on 4- to 6-inch blocks, or use a wedge-shape support to raise just the upper half of your body. (Beware: Sleeping on extra pillows that elevate only your head can aggravate the condition.)

Heaters, Portable

A portable electric heater can warm a room or a corner of a room when you want to keep the house thermostat at a lower-than-normal setting, or when the apartment is not warm enough. A heater lets you work in an unheated basement on a midwinter project, and it provides some emergency heat if your furnace breaks down.

Most heaters have a 1,500-watt maximum output. That's the highest you can safely use in a typical 15-ampere circuit. If one of the rooms you need to warm is small, buy a heater with at least one setting that's lower than 1,500 watts. You may find it comfortable to run the heater at that lower wattage.

Convection heaters use coils to warm the air nearby, which circulates, often aided by a built-in fan. Some models oscillate to spread warmed air over a wider area. Sizes and shapes vary. Most models are small enough to fit on a table, but some heaters are quite small—no more than 10 inches on a side—and are convenient for under-desk use.

Liquid-filled heaters resemble an old-fashioned upright radiator. The liquid inside (typically oil) warms up slowly. These units are heavy and usually mounted on casters.

Radiant heaters have an electric coil or a quartz tube that radiates heat directly to objects—i.e., people—in its line of sight. A radiant heater gives fast spot heating (for example, if you've just gotten out of bed in a chilly room, the focused heating of a radiant model can quickly warm you while you dress in front of it) but leaves the room air almost as cool as when you got up. This is primarily useful for a cold basement or garage—it warms you long before a convection heater could warm the whole area.

Herbal Supplements

Herbal dietary supplements are sometimes expensive, they may mislead you with false promises, and they offer no assurances that what's on the label is what's inside. If you want to try a supplement despite the uncertainties, don't rely on what's printed on the packages or in pamphlets. Do your best to seek out independent sources of information about what the herbs and other supplements are supposed to do. Two books have been recommended. Both are by Varro Tyler, an expert in the medicinal use of plants: *The Honest Herbal—a Sensible Guide to the Use of Herbs and Related Remedies* (third edition, 1993) and *Herbs of Choice— The Therapeutic Use of Phytomedicinals* (1994). Both are published by Pharmaceutical Products Press (Haworth).

Here are some other suggestions for playing it safe:

- Before trying a supplement, consider changes to your diet or lifestyle that might accomplish your goals. If you have high cholesterol, for example, cut your intake of saturated fat and begin an exercise program before you consider taking garlic pills.

- Check with your doctor before taking an herb or other supplement. Many people don't, for fear of looking silly or getting a lecture. But it's worth the risk of embarrassment. A supplement may interact with a drug you take or cause a serious side effect, and the doctor may know of an effective conventional treatment you should try first.

- Pregnant and nursing women and anyone with chronic and serious health problems should not take herbal supplements unless their doctor approves.

- Check the warnings on packages and on related material. Start with small doses.

- Buy herbs that at least claim to be "standardized," so you have a fighting chance of consistent contents from pill to pill.

- Stick to single-herb products, not combinations, whose actions might be hard to sort out.

- Be alert to the herb's effects, positive and negative. If you can track progress objectively—with cholesterol tests, say, or by keeping tabs on your urinary flow if you're taking a prostate remedy—you'll be less susceptible to the power of suggestion.

- Stop immediately if there's a problem, and call the doctor. For instance, abdominal pain, darkened urine, and jaundice can signal liver complications that an herb may have brought on.

If you think a product made you sick, the Food and Drug Administration (FDA) advises you to contact your doctor, who should then call the agency's MedWatch hotline. The agency also suggests contacting your state and local health departments and consumer protection agency.

Homeowner's Insurance

The cost of insuring your home depends not only on the type of policy you choose but on where you live and what you live in. Insurance companies base their rates for homeowner's policies on a number of factors.

Location. Companies keep records of the claims they've had to pay, dividing territory by cities, zip codes, and even neighborhoods, to determine the risk of insuring homes. Residents of areas with traditionally high losses—from crime, fires, or natural disasters—can expect to pay more than residents of low-loss areas.

Fire-protection class. How close is your home to the nearest fire station. How well trained are the firefighters? The closer you are and the better they're trained, the lower your premiums should be. An industry advisory organization assigns every neighborhood in the United States a fire-protection class, based on the quality of fire protection and the distance of homes from a water source. (Some large insurance companies use their own rating systems.) For that reason, a rural home miles from a fire station may cost more to insure than an urban home in a higher-crime area but around the corner from a firehouse.

Type of building. Wooden houses cost 5–10 percent more to insure than brick ones, which withstand fire better. Earthquake insurance, however, costs considerably less for wood-frame homes, which tend to withstand quakes better than brick.

Age of home. Companies may charge up to 20 percent less to insure new homes than to insure older ones, which may be more susceptible to damage in storms and fires. Outdated building standards and old wiring can also make older homes riskier to insure.

Number of units. Companies may charge more to insure apartments or condominiums in large buildings than in small ones because the risk of fire increases with the number of occupants.

Deductibles and discounts

Although there's little you can do to change the location or basic construction of your house, you may be able to reduce the cost of your premium in other ways. By raising your deductible from $250 to $1,000, for instance, you may be able to reduce your yearly premium by a significant amount. Many insurance companies also offer discounts to homeowners who meet certain qualifications. When shopping for a new homeowner's-insurance policy or reviewing your current coverage, don't overlook these discounts.

Multiple-policy discounts. Many insurance companies that write auto, homeowner's, and umbrella policies offer discounts of 5–15 percent to customers who keep two or more policies with them.

Smoke-detector and burglar-alarm discounts. Most companies offer discounts of 2–5 percent for homes with smoke detectors or burglar alarms. The more effective the security system, the higher the discount. Some companies may cut your premium by up to 20 percent if you install an in-house sprinkler system or a very sophisticated burglar-alarm system. Not every system qualifies for the discount, so it's worth checking with your insurance company before you buy any costly security device.

Fire-resistant house discounts. A few insurers offer discounts of up to 15 percent for homes made of fire-resistant materials.

Nonsmoker discounts. A few insurers offer discounts to homeowners who don't smoke.

Mature-homeowner's discounts. Some companies offer discounts of up to 10 percent to homeowners who are at least 50 to 55 years old and retired.

Longtime-customer discounts. Some insurers offer discounts to customers who have maintained coverage with them for several years.

Home Theater

A "home theater" can be as simple as a VCR hooked up to a TV set or as complex as a projection TV wired to a couple of VCRs, a laser-disc player, and a sound system with multiple loudspeakers customized for a room's acoustics.

Before you go shopping, figure out which features are important to you. Be prepared for a sales pitch to get you to buy higher in the line than you intend, and be wary of sales "expertise." The salespeople may not know any more about the product than you do, and they may have a vested interest in selling you particular brands in stock.

Don't buy an extended warranty—it's a bad investment. If solid-state circuitry fails, it usually fails early, within 90 days or so—when the manufacturer's own warranty is likely to be in effect. Extended warranties usually don't cover belts and other parts that wear out with heavy use, nor do they cover accidental breakage. Prepare yourself for a hard sell, since stores make a hefty profit from these contracts. If you feel you need some protection, make your purchase with one of the credit cards that doubles the manufacturer's warranty for a maximum period of up to one year.

Hotel Security

If you're concerned about safety when staying at a hotel, do a security check before settling in for the night. (At some hotels, you may be able to check even before you register.) The door to your room should have a deadbolt lock. It should also have a peephole. The door to any adjoining room should also have a deadbolt lock. Windows that could be accessible from the outside should have a strong lock, sliding glass doors, and a bar.

The hallways of the hotel should have no blind corridors or other hiding places. The corridors should be well lighted. If the corridor doors can be opened only with a room key, so much the better.

Look for other clues as well. A hotel that's concerned about security will never give out guests' names or room numbers. Room keys won't be piled up on maids' carts in the hallways, or at the front desk.

Once in your room, never open the door to anyone, even a hotel employee, without first calling the front desk to see whether someone was sent. If you feel uneasy in a particular room, never hesitate to ask to be moved to another.

Humidifiers

A humidifier reduces static electricity; it protects wood furniture and paneling, fabrics, and even computers from damage caused by excessively dry, warm air.

Humidification can make you feel warmer at relatively cool temperatures. It helps protect the respiratory system, aiding the body's defenses against viruses and air pollutants. Moisture from a humidifier can help cold sufferers feel better by reducing dryness and irritation in the nose and throat. Tabletop humidifiers can add moisture to one or two rooms at a time. Console humidifiers can raise the humidity in the entire house.

Ultrasonic and impeller-driven "cool-mist" models spray water directly into the air, often resulting in annoying white dust on furniture and other surfaces. The white dust can be reduced or eliminated if you use distilled water, if you buy an expensive demineralization cartridge, or if you have very soft water. Steam-mist models, also known as vaporizers, can scald if you get too close to the mist they produce or if you tip them over by accident. Their modern cousins, warm-mist vaporizers, also boil water, but the steam is cooled before it comes out of the vaporizer's nozzle. Evaporative models use an absorbent pad to disperse moisture, with the aid of a fan that pulls air through the pad. Most console models are evaporative units.

Cleaning frequency. At a minimum, humidifiers need a daily cold-water rinse and a refill with clean water. The absorbent pad in an evaporative model needs regular rinsing, and may require replacement at least once a year.

To deter the growth of microorganisms and kill off germs, you should disinfect the humidifier weekly, washing it with an ounce of chlorine bleach diluted in a pint of water, then rinsing thoroughly. Or, to avoid the bleachy smell, try one part hydrogen peroxide diluted in 100 parts of water. The peroxide kills most microbes—but it needs to be used every three days.

To get rid of mineral deposits, you should clean the humidifier at least once a week with a soft brush or towel and undiluted white vinegar.

Ice Cream

To make ice cream, manufacturers pasteurize and homogenize a mixture of milk, cream, sweeteners, and other ingredients, then cool the mixture, add flavors and colors, and whip air into it as it freezes. (Fruit, chips, and other chunks are inserted later, just before a final freezing.) The added air results in "overrun," an increase in volume.

A half-cup of ice cream has 120 to 300 calories and from about 5 to 18 grams of fat, about two-thirds of it saturated. At the high end of the range are superpremium ice creams. The low end of the range includes the cheaper supermarket brands.

According to government guidelines for a person eating 2,000 calories a day, a half-cup of regular ice cream provides roughly 10 to 15 percent of the daily limit for total fat and about 20 to 30 percent of the limit for saturated fat. For a serving of superpremium ice cream, double those figures; for many light ice creams, cut them in half.

Before relatively new labeling regulations went into effect, products could only be labeled as "ice cream" if they had at least 10 percent milk fat. Any product with less was required to go by a name such as "ice milk" or "frozen dairy dessert." Now, these products can be called "light ice cream," or, perhaps, "reduced-fat" or "low-fat" ice cream. Whatever the name, if you are counting calories, you still have to read the numbers on the back of the box.

Frozen yogurt. Most regular frozen yogurts bear a close nutritional resemblance to ice cream: They generally have at least some fat, and their sugar content can give them as many calories as ice cream. The boundaries between frozen yogurt and ice cream have blurred still further with the blending of candies, swirls, and chunks of cookies and pies into frozen yogurts.

Sherbets and ices. Sherbets and ices fall somewhere between low-fat and nonfat. They have one to two percent milk fat, with perhaps a gram of fat per half-cup serving. But because sherbet is generally denser than ice cream and has more sweetener, it's not always especially low in calories.

Ices and sorbets, also high in sugar, contain no dairy ingredients and have little or no fat. Sorbets generally have fewer calories per serving than sherbets.

Iced Tea

You'd expect ready-to-drink tea to taste like freshly brewed iced tea flavored with fresh-squeezed lemon or other fresh fruit and sweetened to taste. Unfortunately, according to trained taste panelists convened by Consumers Union, most ready-to-drink tea has a weak, nondescript flavor.

Canned tea may produce a harsh throat-burn sensation caused by the presence of preservatives such as sodium or potassium benzoate and sodium sorbate.

If you want the best-tasting iced tea, you'll have to brew it yourself.

Impotence

Although stress, anxiety, or depression can contribute to impotence (erectile dysfunction), they're usually not the primary cause. (Occasional difficulty achieving or maintaining an erection, which becomes increasingly frequent with age, is not considered true impotence.) The problem is much more likely to stem from medical factors, such as drug side effects, impaired circulation, neurological problems, or hormonal imbalance. If psychological factors really are to blame, counseling by a sex therapist or treatment for depression may help. When physiological or psychological treatment fails to correct the underlying problem, men can try a number of mechanical techniques for creating an erection, including drug injections, constricting bands, vacuum pumps, and surgical implants.

Insect Repellents

Most insect repellents are based on N, N-diethyl-meta-toluamide, a chemical that goes by the nickname deet. Because deet is so successful at repelling mosquitoes and flies, users may be tempted to slather themselves with the stuff. That's not a good idea. Deet is readily absorbed into the bloodstream, and medical reports have shown that absorption of deet sometimes has neurological consequences. A common side effect is a rash that can occur in people with sensitive skin. To see if you're susceptible, apply a small amount to your forearm, then check for redness over the next day or two.

Despite deet's effectiveness, it's wise to avoid unnecessary exposure to the chemical. You can do that in several ways:

- Use a low-deet repellent and apply it sparingly. (Products with 20–40 percent deet are effective when the equivalent of two to four tablespoons are used for arms, legs, and face.) If bugs don't respond to a thin film of repellent, use a bit more.

- Don't apply repellent near eyes, on lips, or on broken skin. (To apply spray to your face, spray your palm, then spread the repellent carefully.)

- Avoid breathing a repellent spray, and don't use it near food.

- Once it's not needed, wash repellent off with soap and water.

- On children, use a product containing less than 20 percent deet, and keep it out of their reach. Don't apply repellent to a young child's hands, which often wind up in the mouth.

- Consider treating your clothes instead of your skin. But note that deet can damage spandex, rayon, and acetate.

Lyme disease

Although Lyme disease, spread by the deer tick, has received a lot of publicity and is serious, it may not warrant all the hoopla that has surrounded it. Still, it's a good idea to minimize your chances of infection. Some makers of insect repellents would have you believe that deet is all you need, but deet products don't do a good job of repelling deer ticks.

There are other products that can help dramatically. They contain 0.5 percent permethrin. It also kills mosquitoes and biting flies. Permethrin is relatively safe for people—it is used in higher concentrations, in prescription products, to treat head lice and scabies.

Permethrin spray isn't meant to be applied to the skin, where the chemical breaks down; it's meant for use on clothes, shoes, tents, netting, and sleeping bags. Spray only enough to moisten the material, spray only on the outside of clothes, and let clothes dry for at least two hours before you wear them. One treatment should last through a few washings.

There are other, nonchemical precautions to take when venturing into tick country:

- Tuck pants cuffs into boots or socks.

- Stay to the center of hiking paths, avoiding tall grass.

- Inspect yourself after leaving an infested area. Deer ticks are hard to see—nymphs are dot-size; adults, smaller than a sesame seed—so you'll need to look closely.

If you discover a tick feasting away despite your best efforts to repel it, don't panic: An infected tick doesn't usually transmit the Lyme organism during the first 24 hours. Remove the tick with tweezers, grasping it close to the skin and applying steady upward pressure to make sure all parts of the tick are removed from your skin. Then disinfect the area with rubbing alcohol or povidine iodine (Betadine). You may want to save the tick in alcohol for later identification, should you become sick.

Insomnia

If you can't sleep because of emotional distress or jet lag, taking sleeping pills for a short time (no more than two weeks) may help you get some rest.

In other cases of sleeplessness, it's better to identify and treat the underlying cause. For example, sleep can be disrupted by indigestion, or by frequent urination induced by an enlarged prostate. Insomnia also can be caused by common drugs such as beta-blockers and decongestants.

Among the most common causes of chronic insomnia are poor sleep habits. Your sleep may improve if you exercise in the late afternoon or early evening; avoid daytime naps; don't use the bedroom for working, eating, or watching television; don't eat or drink just before bed; use relaxation techniques to help fall asleep; and get up at the same time each day, including weekends.

If you just can't fall asleep, try staying awake instead. Based on the premise that the anxiety of "trying" to sleep can itself keep you awake, the counterintuitive technique is one of the strategies that sleep specialists sometimes recommend.

Insurance Policy Cancellation

An insurance company may cancel your policy after only a couple of claims. However, insurers must follow the guidelines established by each state for cancelling insurance policies. If the claims are your fault, the insurance company has a right to increase the policy's rate or decline to renew the policy. If fraud is involved, it may cancel your policy before the renewal date. If you think you have been treated unfairly, it's appropriate to call the state insurance department for guidance.

International Driving

If you plan to rent a car in Europe, you may need an International Driving Permit (IDP). Basically, the IDP is a translation of your regular U.S. or Canadian license, not a license in its own right. You still need your regular license. The IDP fulfills a requirement that you carry a version of your license that can be read by a local police or traffic official if you're stopped. You normally don't need to show an IDP to rent a car, but you may need to show one when you operate it.

You don't, of course, need an IDP when you drive in a country where English is the main language. Several European countries—notably the Scandinavian and Benelux ones, the Czech Republic, France, and Switzerland—also don't require one. But you may be required to show an IDP in Austria, Germany, Greece, Italy, Spain, and most of Eastern Europe. A travel agent, your local automobile association affiliate, or the visitor bureau of your destination can provide you with the specific requirements of individual countries.

If you have any doubt, get an IDP. They're available for $10 from the 1,000 or so AAA travel agencies (you needn't be an AAA member) and for C$10 from any CAA office. The minimum age is 18; you'll need a valid U.S. or Canadian license and two passport-size photos.

Investing $50 or Less

Here are a few ways to invest $50 or less, listed in order of relative ease:

Pay off your credit cards. If you carry a credit-card balance, chipping away at it should be your first priority. Paying off the balance on a credit card that charges yearly interest at a high double-digit rate is as good as earning that same rate of interest on an investment.

Invest where you work. If your employer offers a 401(k) or other defined-contribution plan and you're not already putting in as much as you're allowed to, consider increasing your contribution. You'll reduce next year's income-tax bill and you'll have more set aside when you retire. Your employer may also match some or all of your contribution.

Buy U.S. Savings Bonds. Series EE Savings Bonds sell for half their face value. Although savings bonds are unlikely ever to reward you with spectacular returns, they're among the safest of investments. Savings bonds are available at most banks and through automatic payroll deductions at many companies.

Buy stock directly. If you already own stock and participate in a dividend-reinvestment plan (through which the dividends you earn are automatically reinvested to buy more shares), you may be able to make additional cash contributions whenever you wish. Many dividend investment plans accept checks as small as $10 or $25.

Prepay your mortgage. You may be able to save a substantial amount of interest over the term of your mortgage and pay it off years earlier by making relatively small prepayments of principal along the way. For example, if you were to pay an additional $50 a month on a 30-year $100,000 mortgage at 9 percent interest, you would save $49,434 in interest and pay off the mortgage 6½ years earlier.

Before you start sending money, call your lender for its rules on prepaying mortgages. Not all lenders will accept prepayments, except in states where they are required to. Some lenders may also want separate checks for prepayments. If you decide to prepay, be sure to keep your canceled checks to help settle any future differences of opinion.

J

Jack Stands

No matter how good your jack, you shouldn't bet your life on its support alone while you're working near or underneath a car. Once the car is jacked up, support it with jack stands. Even some ramp manufacturers recommend stands as a backup. That may seem to be too much, but it's smart to use a belt-and-suspenders approach when as much as two tons of steel are hovering over you.

There are stands that ratchet their way upward by means of grooves in their column and those that are held in place by a steel pin you insert through holes in the base and column. Ratcheting stands offer more height settings than the pin type, and they are the easiest type to adjust. Once the car is jacked up and the stand placed under the frame, you merely lift the column as high as you'd like. When you let go, it will automatically lock into place at the nearest lower position.

With a pin-type stand, you lift the column with one hand, make sure the hole in the base lines up with the appropriate hole in the column, then use the other hand to insert the locking pin through the aligned holes. Once a car is being supported, neither type of stand can be made to drop it. To lower the car, you jack the car up a bit, slip the stand out, and operate the jack's release valve.

As stable as jack-stand bases are on hard, level surfaces, most have legs that dig into soft surfaces like warm asphalt. A sinking stand could not only damage a driveway; it could cause the load to shift and maybe even fall. To make any jack more stable and less apt to gouge soft surfaces, put a board under its legs.

K

Kidney Stones

Kidney-stone sufferers may be told to stay on a low-oxalate diet. The richest food sources of oxalate are spinach, cocoa, parsley, rhubarb, and tea. Lesser, but still significant, amounts are found in green beans, carrots, and celery. Cutting down on these foods may help to reduce stone formation if you have a history of kidney stones composed of calcium oxalate. For anyone with a history of kidney stones, it's also very important to keep the urine well diluted by drinking lots of fluids.

L

Laundry Detergents, Bleaches

Detergents containing bleach or "bleach alternative" shouldn't need any help getting clothes clean. You don't have to add bleach to perk up a load of whites, but it won't do any harm. Bleaches oxidize stains and soils, loosening them to make it easier for a detergent to lift them from the clothes.

Liquid chlorine bleaches, all of which use the same chemical, whiten, sanitize, and deodorize laundry. They are usually safe to use on cotton, linen, and washable synthetics except spandex. And they work best if added five minutes into the wash cycle, to give the detergent time to begin its work. Chlorine bleaches should not be used on wool, silk, leather, or mohair, and they may not be safe on colored fabrics.

Unlike chlorine bleaches, oxygen bleaches keep laundry white but can't make it white. They are safe for most colored washables; check the clothing labels. Don't use chlorine and oxygen bleaches together. Do a colorfastness test before using any bleach.

Laundry Detergents, Concentrated

The little containers of superconcentrated or "ultra" powders and liquids that have taken over the supermarket shelves are as effective as conventional detergents. Any one of them should get ordinary soiled clothes as clean as you'd like. As a class, concentrated powders outperform concentrated liquids.

Lawn Blowers

If possible, choose an electric blower rather than an inherently noisy gasoline-powered model. An electric makes less noise—and there is less danger from fuel spills or fingers scorched on hot engine surfaces. A typical gasoline-powered blower is so loud that using one requires wearing ear protectors.

Any extension cord you use with an electric blower must be intended for outdoor use, which means it will have heavy-duty construction. The cord must also have a three-prong grounding plug and connector if the blower requires that kind of a connection. Chances are, however, that a new blower will have so-called double insulation and you won't need a three-conductor extension cord. For big lawn-cleaning jobs, you may want to consider a homeowner version of the gasoline-powered machines lawn-care services use.

A gasoline-powered backpack model may be an alternative to a hand-held model (gas or electric). Once donned and properly adjusted, a 20-pound backpack blower isn't nearly as fatiguing to use as a hand-held blower. But they cost a great deal more and are noisier.

Lawn Mowers

Whatever mower you use, you'll get the best results if you:

• Keep the cutting blade sharp—torn grass will turn brown.

• Change your mowing route occasionally, so the grass doesn't show a pattern.

• Set the cutting height to remove no more than the top third of the grass.

• Water generously but only about once a week or so.

Manual mowers. These don't have any complicated controls, no elaborate safety precautions, no maintenance aside from occasional sharpening or blade adjustment, no loud noise, and no fuel requirements. Add low cost to those advantages and it's clear why these mowers have made a comeback. Unfortunately, most manual mowers are effective only when the grass height is 3 inches or less. The maximum cutting height is 1½ inches. They can't cut closer than 3 inches from obstacles. Their handles rest at an uncomfortably low position. A grass catcher is impractical. But a manual mower does have one big advantage: They are a boon for people who want the exercise.

Electric mowers. Like manual mowers, electric mowers are quiet, require little maintenance, and are often inexpensive. Otherwise, they're a lot like gas mowers. Both types use a rotary blade and offer a choice of cutting modes. Their chief constraint, a trailing electric cord (typically a long, heavy-duty extension cord that plugs into a 15-ampere outlet), is avoided in cordless, battery-powered mowers. But when you substitute battery power for regular electric power from a household outlet, the price goes up. The area you can cover goes down—one-fourth to one-half an acre, depending on the brand and model. Charging the battery may take 16–24 hours.

Gas mowers. Push-type gas mowers, in which the engine spins the cutting blade but doesn't drive the mower wheels, are the most widely used mowers in the United States. That's no surprise—some cost less than $100. Self-propelled mowers start at about twice as much.

In general, a power mower that collects grass clippings in a side bag is better at spreading clippings than it is at bagging them. Side-baggers typically come with a discharge chute; a catcher costs extra. Rear-baggers are usually good at bagging clippings and at least adequate at dispersing them. Rear-baggers typically come with a catcher; a chute is extra.

Mulch? A homeowner with a half-acre lawn winds up with as

much as three tons of grass clippings a year. Clippings and other lawn debris put out with the trash make up nearly one-fifth of the material dumped in landfills. One sensible alternative to dumping clippings is to use a mower that mulches. Mulched grass decomposes easily, returning nutrients to the soil. Another alternative is to compost grass clippings with other yard waste.

Lipstick

While lipsticks still promise up-to-the-minute lip fashion, many also claim to moisturize, condition, and protect lips from the sun and wind.

This "treatment" approach is not a bad idea. Lips are different from the rest of the skin on the face and body; they're more like an extension of the inside of the mouth. Most skin has a layer of dead cells to protect it from the elements and slow the loss of moisture, but lips don't. Moreover, lips lack pores and sebaceous glands, so they can't produce oily secretions to moisturize themselves. As a result, lips are vulnerable to drying, chapping, and cracking.

Lips are also quite vulnerable to sun damage. Lipstick alone is opaque enough to provide a little protection from the sun, but many manufacturers boost that protection by adding sunscreen.

Loans for the Self-Employed

People who are self-employed commonly have income that varies from year to year. They may worry about qualifying for a mortgage and turn to a "no-income-verification" loan. As a first step, it's better to try and obtain a traditional loan. No-income-verification loans don't require the borrower to provide documentation of income, but they do require a substantial down payment (20 percent or more), and the interest rate is slightly higher, too.

Long-Distance Calls

If you use your telephone company calling card to call long distance, you don't necessarily pay the rate charged by the company that issued your card. The rate you pay often depends on the price charged by the independent carrier that operates the phone from which you are calling. Simply using your calling card won't allow you to bypass the independent carrier. To route the call through your normal carrier, you need to dial its access code (for example, 1-0-ATT-0 in the case of AT&T).

Loudspeakers

Speakers come in many shapes, sizes, and prices. Conventional speakers priced at $300–$400 per pair deliver the best combination of price and quality. When you pay more, you usually buy better bass and nicer cabinets.

There are "audio" models, sold in pairs, and "video" models, sold in systems of three or five speakers. In addition, for home theater, speakers are sold singly for use as center-channel speakers and in pairs of inexpensive small models for use as rear "ambience" speakers. Much of the difference between speakers meant for a sound system and those sold as video systems is packaging: You can put together a fine sound system for home theater from regular speakers. Most speakers have a woofer for bass and a tweeter and sometimes a midrange driver for the rest of the music spectrum. Satellite systems generally are composed of a bass module and two small, easy-to-place satellite speakers, which reproduce only the midrange and the treble. In-wall speakers are recessed into household walls to save space. Powered speakers have built-in amplifiers.

Buying advice. Be sure you can return or exchange speakers that don't sound as good in your home as in the showroom. Thick speaker cable (16 gauge or lower) is better than the thin, high-gauge wire often provided with speakers, especially if the cable is long.

Speaker placement. For music only, speakers should form a triangle with the listener; a satellite system's subwoofer can be placed unobtrusively behind furniture. For home theater, put a center speaker near or atop the TV set; rear speakers flank the listener.

Luggage, Soft-Sided

Some soft-sided cases, aimed mainly at airplane travelers, are designed to hold a separate carry-on bag piggyback style. The duffel bag is another soft-sided luggage variety. Pullman cases are preferable to duffel bags for those who want their clothes to stay neat. For casual travelers, who don't mind carrying their luggage instead of wheeling it, a duffel is more convenient than a Pullman.

Shell. Many bags have a nylon or polyester shell; others use a shell of "ballistic" fabric, made from fibers similar to those in bulletproof vests. Ballistic fabrics are preferable because they resist tearing better than other fabrics. As an alternative, choose nylon or polyester yarns of at least 1,000 denier. (Denier refers to the yarn size; the larger the number, the heavier the yarn.)

Capacity. A soft-sided bag's fabric shell stretches to accommodate bulky loads. Bags of at least 2 cubic feet can carry a week's worth of clothing with a few inches of space to spare.

Frame. As a rule, a full metal frame can more easily be deformed than a plastic one.

Pockets, pouches, straps. Most bags have at least one small pocket or pouch on the inside, useful for holding hosiery, underwear, and such. Many Pullman cases also have straps to help keep clothes from shifting and wrinkling once they are packed.

Handles. Shoulder straps and handles connected by rivets are likely to prove more durable than those fastened with D-shaped rings and screws. On duffel bags, two handles absorb the bag's weight better than one long shoulder strap. On Pullmans, retractable pull handles are better than detachable ones, which can easily get lost in transit.

Zippers. Most soft-siders have "self-repairing" zippers, the kind that can be linked together again even if a stray piece of clothing gets snagged in the teeth or if a too-full bag forces the zipper apart.

Seams and bindings. Check for narrow seam edges or bulky seam binding—signs that the seams may not hold. Also, the closer the stitches, the better. A bag with leather edge bindings, or trimmed with shell fabric or wide woven tape, holds up to abrasion better than one with plastic trim on the edges.

Wheels. If you often travel by plane, look for a bag with wheels protected by housings or partly recessed in the base of the bag. This type of construction tends to shield the wheels from rough handling. Bags with four wheels are much easier to use than those with two. Two-wheeled bags have a habit of banging into ankles, knees, and legs during use. Moreover, the full weight of a two-wheeled bag strains the pulling arm.

M

Mail-Order Shopping

When ordering by mail order, sometimes the postage and handling charges may seem excessive. There are no specific laws that govern what a company can charge for postage and handling. However, the Federal Trade Commission has rules that say companies cannot misrepresent costs to consumers. That means what companies tell you is the cost of postage and handling must be the maximum you're subsequently charged for those items. The practice of blending postage and handling in a single charge leaves consumers with little idea of where the money actually goes. For example, it's difficult to ascertain how much of the amount will eventually go to the postal service or shipping company and how much will be retained by the mail-order company to help cover its costs, from overhead to labor to packaging materials.

Microwave Ovens

Large ovens have a claimed capacity of more than a cubic foot. Midsize models' capacity is just under a cubic foot. Nearly all come with a turntable, a feature to help a microwave oven cook uniformly.

The higher the wattage, the faster the cooking. Today's midsize and large ovens deliver 800 to 1,050 watts at full power.

Look for a timed reheat setting that can be adjusted to serving size. It's useful to have a moisture sensor, which gauges when the proper amount of moisture has escaped from a loosely covered dish and turns the oven off automatically.

An important use for a microwave oven is defrosting. Most ovens have an automatic defrost feature. Typically, you enter the weight of the food on the control panel; some ovens also prompt you to specify whether the food is meat, poultry, or fish. The oven then calculates the power level and defrosting time.

Despite a special popcorn setting, you may get better results simply by following the instructions on the popcorn package.

Helpful controls

Some features, such as two-stage cooking or timed-delay start, aren't as useful as some other controls.

Cooking time entry. Most ovens have ten numbered electronic touchpads plus two or more special touchpads for reheating, defrosting, and other tasks. Ordinarily, to set a heating time, you enter it directly: 2, 3, 8 for 2 minutes and 38 seconds. But with a few ovens, you enter that time by tapping a 1-minute pad once, a 10-second pad three times, and a 1-second pad eight times.

Instant-on touchpads. These make it easier to use a special setting; you don't also have to touch Time or Start to get things started.

Shortcut touchpads. With most models, you can punch in the time you want by tapping a single touchpad. With some ovens, you can also tap in extra minutes to extend the time of a setting that's already on, even at a low-power setting.

Many ovens have settings for cooking specific foods, such as potatoes or muffins and rolls. Typically, these settings time the cooking automatically. Ovens with a moisture sensor can reheat food almost perfectly. The sensor is also useful for other tasks, such as cooking vegetables.

Microwaving Produce

Any cooking method robs fruits and vegetable of vitamins. To minimize the losses, minimize the length of time that produce spends exposed to heat or water. Your best bet: Microwave the food, tightly covered, no longer than necessary, and in just enough water to prevent burning—about 1 teaspoon per two servings. Be sure to allow for the recommended "standing" time after the microwave shuts off so the steam can finish the cooking.

Milk, Acidophilus

Acidophilus milk has had *Lactobacillus acidophilus* bacteria added to it. It has the same nutritional value as milk without the bacteria. Some people believe that it is good for digestive upsets, or can help combat lactose intolerance, but several studies have failed to document this.

Moisturizers, Facial

Think of the skin as a multilayered stack of fluffed-up pillows (the living cells, supplied with moisture by blood vessels) topped by several layers of deflated pillows (the dead cells of the stratum corneum, or horny layer). The skin constantly renews itself. New cells are produced deep in the living layers, while dead cells are pushed toward the surface, where they lose their moisture and flatten out. Eventually, they're sloughed off.

The moisture in the skin's living cells passes into the air, especially if the air is dry. If the skin loses water too fast, its top layer dries out and may even crack, and fine wrinkles appear.

The skin has its own way of trying to hold onto moisture: Its glands produce oily substances that slow the passage of water. These glands are more active in men and young women than they are in older women. As a result, older women are apt to be especially bothered by dry skin and may need to rely on a moisturizer.

Moisturizers penetrate the stratum corneum, but they don't get into the living skin underneath. (The stratum corneum is the part that dries out, so they don't *need* to get farther down.)

They counteract dryness in two ways: "Occlusive" types, such as petroleum jelly, physically block moisture from leaving the skin; "humectant" types, such as glycerin, attract moisture from the skin and the surrounding air and thereby slow down the rate of loss. Most moisturizers use both kinds of ingredients, mixed with water. Products made especially for dry skin have more oil than others and may feel greasier. Products for oily skin may use only humectants and leave less residue than others.

Alpha-hydroxy acids (AHAs), derived from fruit, milk, and sugarcane, have a reputation for making wrinkles disappear. When they're applied in great enough amounts—in chemical peels, say—they can make skin shed dead cells more rapidly and increase its moisture content. Such changes can make wrinkles less evident, and can help treat acne or other skin damage. But most cosmetics that contain AHAs have them in small concentrations, and their effectiveness is untested.

Although there is anecdotal evidence that some moisturizers with AHAs reduce fine wrinkles, the many products on the market use different ingredients in different concentrations. If you're thinking about using AHAs, it's best to ask a dermatologist's advice. If you're already using a product with AHAs and it starts to irritate your skin, stop using it.

Liposomes are microscopic particles made from fatty substances, some of which occur naturally in the skin. Liposomes hold a moisturizing material and theoretically carry it deeper into the skin than a simple smear of the same material would. But no moisturizer gets into living cells.

Ceramides are similar to natural lipids in the topmost layer of skin. Some brands claim to lubricate that layer, as lipids do. But then, so does petroleum jelly.

Collagen and *elastin* are proteins found under the top layer of skin that tend to deteriorate with age or sun damage. But the protein molecules added to moisturizers are too large to penetrate the skin.

Some products are labeled as nonfragranced, hypoallergenic, or noncomedogenic (won't clog pores, causing blackheads), but no label is a guarantee. In fact, several "nonfragranced" products contain aromatics such as sandalwood oil or lavender essence, which may not have been added as fragrances but which impart a slight scent nevertheless.

Mouthwash, Fluoridated

Some people may feel that a fluoridated mouthwash is beneficial for the teeth. In fact, unless one's dentist recommends extra fluoride because of a high risk of dental decay, there's enough fluoride in a fluoridated toothpaste and fluoridated drinking water to supply typical adult needs for fluoride.

Muscle Sprains

*R*est, *i*ce, *c*ompression, and *e*levation (RICE) all help heal a sprain, but the most important step to minimize damage and speed recovery is to apply ice immediately. Cold constricts blood vessels and thus helps prevent swelling.

If you don't have a flexible ice pack, use a bag of frozen vegetables. (Crushed ice soon turns into a frozen block.) Ice the injury for 10 to 20 minutes every hour or two for the first 6–12 hours—at least until the swelling is no longer increasing. If swelling resumes, apply ice again. After a day or two of RICE, gently stretch the injured muscle throughout the day for several days.

Mutual Funds

Stock funds have outperformed most other investments over time, but always with some risk to investors' money. Over any month, year, or even several years, a stock fund's shares may fall in value.

Money you can't live without has no place in the stock market. Before investing in stock funds, it's wise to make sure that you have enough money safely set aside to handle an unexpected financial emergency. Households that depend on the income of one wage earner should try to build up an emergency fund equal to at least six months of essential living expenses; households with two wage earners can probably make do with three months' worth, assuming at least one wage earner has a secure job. Money-market mutual funds, federally insured bank accounts, and short-term bond funds are good safe harbors for your emergency funds.

Building a portfolio. Whatever fund or funds you select, try to build a balance. People with 20 years to go before retirement might put 55 percent of their money in stock funds, 35 percent in bond funds, and the remaining 10 percent in a money-market fund or bank CDs. As they move closer to retirement, they can gradually shift some money out of stock funds and into their less-risky investments. These percentages are based on a common asset-allocation model that suggests people subtract their age from 100 and invest that percentage of their money in stocks, with the rest going into bonds and money-market funds.

Investment counseling

If you find you need more help in choosing funds than is available in specialized publications, don't sign up with the first adviser you encounter. Sound investment advice may well be as close as your neighborhood bank, but how can you tell?

Unfortunately, the fact that your bank may call its salesperson a financial planner means little. Anyone can call themselves a financial planner and offer investment advice. A Certified Financial Planner has passed a course of study and received a certificate. However, even such a person may not be equipped to make appropriate investment recommendations.

Good financial planning should start with a written list of your current assets, debts, and income. The adviser should ask about your goals: when you'd like to retire and with what level of income, how you plan to finance your children's education, your tax situation, and so on.

With those factors in mind, the adviser can present a variety of investments with varying risk levels. He or she should be willing to explain each of them to your satisfaction and to let you choose what's best for you.

Insurance agents, lawyers, accountants, and tax preparers may do financial planning. Speak to several before you hand over any money. Shun those who want you to decide immediately. And don't rely on oral representations—get everything in writing.

If you want to pay for investment advice, consider hiring a fee-only financial planner. Such planners charge by the hour and don't make money from commissions. That doesn't mean their advice will always be better, but at least they won't have a vested interest in selling you the products that make them the most in commissions.

N

Nail Care

Cuticles should be pushed back gently with an orange stick wrapped in cotton. Help prevent infected cuticles by not cutting them. Don't use chemical cuticle removers. Cuticle creams and moisturizers are acceptable.

Nails, like hair, are dead tissue. Therefore, be suspicious of products that promise to nourish or condition nails. A paint-on nail strengthener or polish provides only superficial strength. Once the material is removed, nails will be as soft as before. Note: Pale, whitish, or bluish nails may be caused by a medical problem.

Polishing nails. Shape with an emery board. Don't file too low on either side. File from sides to center, in one direction only. Wash hands in soapy water, using a nail brush. Shake polish bottle. Use three polishing strokes; one down the center followed by one on each side. The thinner the coat, the quicker the drying.

O

Oranges and Orange Juice

An orange peel with a green tint simply means the fruit wasn't subjected to a temperature drop while on the tree; inside it may taste as sweet as an orange that lives up to its name.

Fresh orange juice. No packaged juice rivals the taste of fresh-squeezed. The best juice oranges are generally available December through June, although some varieties can be bought as early as October. Avoid navel oranges, which tend to make a bitter juice. Home-squeezed juice may be twice as expensive as a plastic jug of fresh-squeezed juice from the supermarket.

Orange juice nutrition. An eight-ounce glass of orange juice supplies all the vitamin C you need in a day, plus about 7–14 percent of a day's magnesium, potassium, and folate.

P

Paints, Interior Latex

The number of coats you'll have to apply depends on a paint's hiding power, how thickly and smoothly you apply the paint, and the colors involved—the one you've chosen and the one you're covering.

One coat should be able to cover a similar existing color. But drastic transformations, such as changing an orange room to off-white, are more likely to require at least two coats. Generally, the smaller the contrast between old and new, the less critical hiding power will be and the less paint you'll need to make the change.

If you're repainting to cover up scuff marks or to eliminate a mottled or marbleized look that's grown tiresome, you may need to prepare or prime the walls before you apply a new color. Use primer to cover stains, splotches, and repair jobs, which may be too dark for any paint to cover well in one or two coats.

Marbleizing, sponge-painting, and other special effects that yield colors ranging from very light to very dark should be covered with primer, then painted. You can even tint the primer to approximate the new paint color.

Applying paint. Most people prefer the speed and convenience of a roller. When paint makers calculate coverage, they assume it's going to be spread on in a thick layer, using a gallon for 450 square feet or so. But often, users do not apply it thickly enough, spreading the paint at some 650 square feet per gallon or more. The thinner paint film isn't likely to cover adequately in one coat.

If the paint you want claims one-coat coverage, you can estimate the amount of paint needed on the basis of 450 square feet per gallon for one coat. That should give you enough paint, spread at the "normal" rate of 650 square feet, with some left for touch-ups. But if you do run short, take back the old paint can and lid, which has the color recipe and lot number on it, to get the best match. After reloading your roller or brush, start at a new spot and work back to where you just left off, overlapping to make a neat job.

Peanut Butter

Spread on bread, peanut butter is a cheap source of protein, niacin, and folic acid. Three tablespoons spread on two slices of bread provide about as much fiber as a bowl of bran flakes. But take note: The sandwich packs 419 calories and 26 grams of fat (5 grams of it saturated).

If you like peanut butter but want to cut fat from your diet, don't do it by eating a reduced-fat spread. It isn't likely to be very good, and there's a good chance that it will be as high in calories as regular peanut butter. It's better to cut back on fat and calories by spreading a little less of a normal-fat peanut butter.

Peanuts

You don't eat any less fat by choosing dry-roasted nuts over the usual oil-roasted kind. That's because oil-roasted nuts are not immersed in the boiling oil long enough to absorb any of it, and the excess oil is drained off afterward.

Pesticides in Baby Food

The issue of baby-food safety arose recently when environmental groups released test results on eight varieties of baby food. More than half the products contained pesticides—although in all cases the pesticides were at levels well below federal limits.

An expert committee convened by the National Academy of Sciences called for stricter regulation of pesticide residues in the diet, in large part because existing tolerances do not take into consideration the fact that infants and children need wider safety margins than adults do.

Nonetheless, there's no need to stop using baby food. Commercial baby foods generally have both fewer pesticide residues and lower levels of them than are found in most fresh fruits and vegetables from the supermarket.

Pneumonia Vaccination

Pneumonia vaccine (Pneumovax) protects only against pneumonia caused by a bacterium called pneumococcus. It will not protect against pneumonia caused by a virus.

In the years before antibiotics, pneumococcal pneumonia was deadly; today it can be treated effectively in most people. But elderly people, diabetics, and people with chronic heart and lung diseases may be particularly threatened by pneumonia and should be vaccinated at least once every eight years.

Pocket Knives

Pocket knives come in three basic sizes. Pen knives are about 2½ inches long when folded and are popular additions to a key ring. Medium knives are an inch or so longer. They range in complexity from regular models with about 10 tools to top-of-the-line models with a lot of gadgets. Large knives are distinguished by a main blade up to four inches long that locks into place.

How many (and which) tools you want is the first decision to make when buying a pocket knife. A main blade is the standard tool, of course, and your cutting requirements will determine whether you need the long blade found on a large knife or whether a smaller blade will do.

Most owners of a knife equipped with scissors use them fairly often, and the scissors usually operate at least adequately. A standard screwdriver, often included at the tip of a knife's bottle opener, is also useful and versatile. However, most other standbys, including saws, pliers, and wood chisels, lose much of their utility when remade as small, folding pocket-knife tools.

Some other items on pocket knives, such as a can opener or an awl/reamer, tend to be so hard to open that it's unlikely they'll be used much, even if they work well.

Power Drills

A ⅜-inch corded drill, reversible and with variable speed control, is the best choice for beginners and seasoned do-it-yourselfers alike. You can save a few dollars by buying a bare-bones single-speed model, but you sacrifice a lot of versatility. If you decide on a single-speed model, you're better off with a top speed between 1,000 and 1,300 rpm than with a high-speed model. High-speed models drill faster with small bits, but they tend to run too fast with larger bits and most drill accessories. They're also harder to control. There's no significant difference between standard-chuck and keyless-chuck versions.

Most higher-priced corded drills have ball or needle bearings throughout. The cheaper models tend to have sleeve bearings or, at best, a roller-type bearing or two at key stress points around the motor and gear shafts.

Cordless drills are becoming increasingly commonplace, and they're well suited to drilling small holes or driving screws; there's an adjustable slip-clutch that stops driving the screw as soon as the screw head is seated. And they are a lot quieter than corded drills.

There are occasions when a corded drill won't do as well—when working from a ladder or inching through a crawl space, for example, or when you're forced to work where it's wet—in the rain, at poolside, or at a marina. On those occasions, it's a relief not having to think about double insulation or ground faults but simply to know that your drill can't cause an electric shock.

Some cordless models have circuit breakers or special circuitry to protect their components from an overload. Should the drill suddenly get in a bind, one of those devices will trip and interrupt power, usually resetting itself in a matter of seconds.

Look for a battery charger that automatically switches to trickle charge when the batteries become fully charged. That not only prevents the batteries from suffering as a result of overcharging, but it means they don't have to be monitored while they're charging.

Pressure Cookers

Those whose culinary tastes run to legumes and homemade soups and stews might best appreciate a pressure cooker. In minutes, a pressure cooker can create a soup or stew whose rich blend of flavors would otherwise require hours of simmering. Pressure cooking is also the fastest method of all for preparing dried beans and peas, especially if you don't presoak them. Compared with conventional stovetop cooking, pressure cooking consumes less energy and retains more nutrients in food.

However, it takes a little trial and error to get pressure-cooked foods to come out the way you prefer. If you're not prepared to commit the extra time needed to use a pressure cooker, you risk having a cooker gather dust on a top shelf, beside the deep-fat fryer and the hot dog cooker.

R

Receivers

Basic stereo receivers are primarily for people who want to listen to music, although these receivers can also handle audio signals from video components. Dolby Surround Pro Logic models are better suited for handling the soundtrack from a stereo VCR or TV set, or a laser-disc player. Pro Logic receivers convert Dolby Surround soundtracks into separate channels directed to three to five speakers, creating a theaterlike effect. Plain stereo receivers lack Pro Logic circuitry and process the sound with less dramatic effect.

Many Surround receivers offer "ambience" sound processing, which allows you to simulate the acoustics of a concert hall, a nightclub, or the like.

FM receivers range in quality from good to excellent. As long as FM reception is good in your area, you can safely buy by price, type, and features. Examine front-panel controls and displays to see if you can figure which button does what. Look for a model with a simple remote control. And be sure the receiver will work with the impedance requirements of your speakers.

Refrigerators

By the time it has to be replaced at the end of a typical useful life of 15 years, a refrigerator bought new today is likely to have cost about as much to operate as to buy. But that simple parity represents a major improvement in the design of the appliance. Refrigerators have become much more energy efficient. The U.S. Department of Energy requires all refrigerators made after January 1, 1993, to use about 30 percent less electricity than previously. Further tightening of the requirements is anticipated.

Types

Top freezers. More than seven in ten models sold have a top-mounted freezer. They have the widest selection of sizes, styles, and features. They're typically priced lower than other types, and may cost somewhat less to run. Their freezer is at eye level, the most convenient place to find things, but fruits and vegetables stored in low drawers aren't so easy to reach.

Side-by-sides. These are more expensive to buy and run than comparable top-freezers. Many have a through-the-door ice-and-water dispenser. The side-by-side's biggest advantage: You can put at eye level the items you need most often. But narrow shelves make items at the back harder to retrieve. The freezer is slightly larger than in comparable top- and bottom-freezer models.

Bottom freezers. There's not a wide selection available. Some people favor them because all of the refrigerator section is located at a convenient height. Their low freezer is likely to have a pullout basket to make things easier to find, but the basket cuts down a bit on usable space. They can be more expensive to buy than top freezers but may also be cheaper to run.

Built-ins. The most expensive type, typically at least $2,000. The same depth as standard base cabinets (24 inches), they accept front and side panels to match the cabinets. Some come as large as 30 cubic feet.

Compact models. No more than 6 cubic feet, they are handy for a small apartment or a college dorm. The smallest have only about a cubic foot of space. That leaves little room for a freezer compartment.

Feature variety

When it comes to convenience, it's mostly the refrigerator's features that count. Some less-expensive models offer a few of the niceties that follow. High-end models offer these features and more.

With *up-front controls*, you don't have to knock over the ketchup bottle to adjust the thermostat to a colder or warmer setting. *Through-the door ice cube and cold water access* is an advantage, but you'll pay about $250 extra for it, and the refrigerator is more likely to need repairs. An *adjustable meat-keeper* with its own cold-air supply and temperature controls lets you keep meat colder than elsewhere in the refrigerator: that can add a few days to some foods' shelf life. The more *door storage* there is, the less cluttered the interior shelves will be. Many models have room for such bulky items as gallon jugs of milk. *Glass shelves* are easier to keep clean than wire-grid shelves. Some have a sealed, raised lip to contain spills. Some slide out, to help you get things in back. Some refrigerators have a *special crisper* with a control for adjusting humidity in the crisper drawer, a feature that helps keep vegetables from wilting, or keeps fruit fresh. An *ice-maker* is handy to have, but it may require repairs at some point. It also takes up about a cubic foot of prime freezer space. With provision for *adjustable interior space*, movable door-shelf bins add flexibility. Interior shelves can also be rearranged, and some even fold in half to make room for oversize items. Most *dairy bins* have ample room for butter and cheese, and a lid that stays up when raised. *Microwavable containers* provide convenience for storing and heating food. Sliding *door shelf snuggers* are sliding retainers that keep tall bottles from toppling when you open and close the door.

Using a refrigerator efficiently

One way to make a refrigerator less expensive to run is to keep it well stocked with food. That cuts down on the infusion of warm air every time you open the door. Here are some other ways to make the appliance run better:

Plan ahead. If you're redesigning your kitchen, take care not to place the refrigerator right next to the range, or where sunlight will fall on it; otherwise, it will have to work harder to cool.

Clean the coils. They're usually located in the back or on the bottom behind the grill: When they get covered with dust and grime, they can't dissipate heat removed from the refrigerator as well as when they're clean. Many repair calls are solved—at unnecessary expense—by a service technician with a vacuum cleaner.

Check the door gasket. The traditional way (closing the door on a dollar bill and making sure the bill is held tightly) may not work with a magnetic seal. Try this method: Darken the kitchen. Put a brightly-lit flashlight inside the refrigerator, and look for light leaks.

Check temperatures. Buy and use a refrigerator thermometer. Make sure the freezer isn't much colder than 0°F—lower doesn't improve storage life much and adds to energy consumption. While you're at it, the center of the regular storage space should be as close to 37°F as possible. However, it may be tricky to adjust the thermostat to achieve this balance, and the job may have to be done summer and winter, to compensate for large seasonal temperature changes.

Remote Controls

A remote control may be the most important part of an electronic product. It has the potential to try your patience every time you use the component it controls. Fortunately, remotes most likely to get heavy use—those for the TV set and VCR—are likely to have the best design.

A *dedicated* remote, which usually comes with the cheapest TV sets, VCRs, and receivers, operates only the component it comes with. A *unified* remote operates at least one other product of the same brand, although often in a limited way. *Universal* remotes, designed to operate components from a variety of manufacturers, can also serve as a stand-in for a lost or broken remote. A *code-entry* remote comes preprogrammed with the codes for major-brand components and is easy to set up, but it may not support the commands needed for other components that are more than a few years old. A *learning remote* can mimic virtually any command found on other remotes. *Hybrid* models combine both the code-entry and learning features of universal remotes, allowing easy setup and a wide range of functions.

Repairing Appliances

If you know how, and are motivated, there are lots of products that you can fix. For technical assistance, some major appliance manufacturers offer the do-it-yourselfer the most help through toll-free telephone numbers.

If you don't require technical assistance, and the broken product only needs a new stovetop burner, new beaters for a mixer, or a replacement carafe for a coffeepot, it seems simple enough just to buy a new part. Unfortunately, that may not be as simple as it should be. Here's some advice:

- The correct model number is essential. Check the appliance itself; don't rely on manuals or packaging.

- Local stores are the quickest way to get a part. Mass merchandisers and electronics specialty stores are good sources. Parts stores or appliance dealers might also have parts on hand, but you'll have to search the Yellow Pages.

- Contacting the manufacturer may be faster and easier than trying to locate a source yourself. Some companies will sell you the part directly; others will refer you to a parts distributor.

- Phoning a manufacturer is speedier and more effective than writing, particularly if there's any confusion.

- The price of a part for a small appliance may come so close to the price of a new appliance that you may feel that it's easier to pay the small difference and buy a new one. That may feel like a surrender to principle, but the surrender has a lot to do with how much time and patience you have.

Hiring someone to fix it

Choosing the right repairer. There are three basic types of service available:

- Factory service, in which the company maintains its own service center or service fleet.

- Authorized service, consisting of privately run businesses accredited by companies to fix their brands. Sometimes the store that sells the product also acts as an authorized repair service.

- Independents, who set their own policies. Some retailers that offer repairs may fall into this category.

Before you call the repair service or load the ailing device into the car, collect as much documentation as you can find: The owner's manual and the list of repair centers. If the product broke during its warranty period, the sales receipt and warranty statement are important. Once you start the repair process, keep a written record of everything that transpires just in case something goes wrong.

Repairing at home. For emergency repairs such as loss of refrigeration, companies often try to respond within 24 hours. Companies may charge extra for Saturday or evening service calls.

Here are some steps to take:

- Arrange to stay home and watch the work. That way, there will be less temptation for a repairer to do more than is really needed.

- Ask if there's a "trip charge" when setting up the appointment. This charge, typically applied to work that's done out of warranty, includes travel to your home and a minimum labor fee. Expect to pay it, even if you don't go ahead with the work.

- Find out whether you'll pay flat or hourly rates. If the charge is by the hour, find out how it's billed. By the quarter hour is common.

- If you're having a large TV set fixed, ask whether there is a separate transportation charge if the set must be taken back to the shop.

- Ask how long the warranty is, if there is one. Get any warranty in writing.

- Ask to keep any replaced parts. That way, you'll know that a part you are billed for was actually replaced—and the repairer will know that a check on cheating is at least possible.

Repairing in the shop. These steps are similar to what's necessary for home repairs:

- First, get an estimate. Ask whether service includes a standard cleaning or whether it costs extra.

- Ask how long the repair will take. Consumers frequently complain that repairs take longer than the estimate. Ask what the typical waiting time is for parts and whether they have to be ordered from the factory.

- Tell the repairer you will want all replaced parts returned to you.

- Get a claim check that shows the date your product went to the shop and describes the item by brand, model, and serial number. Have the technician or counter clerk sign the check.

- Get detailed receipts for all work and service calls, even if no expense is involved, and a written warranty statement if there is a warranty. Take the names of those you speak with and those who work on the item.

- If you can ship the item without too much trouble, consider factory service. But you'll have to pay for shipping and insurance.

Rollerblading

In-line skating (also known as "rollerblading," after the leading brand) is a growing cause of injuries. The most vulnerable part of the body is the wrist, which bears the brunt of most falls. In addition to wearing wrist guards, wear elbow pads, knee pads, and a helmet.

S

Safe-Deposit Box Insurance

The contents of a safe-deposit box may become damaged if, for example, a below-street-level bank vault becomes flooded. Unless the bank is found to be negligent in some way, it is not responsible for damages. If you have a safe-deposit box, check your contract. If it doesn't cover the box's contents, you may need separate insurance coverage.

In general, items stored in a bank safe-deposit box are covered in a standard homeowner's policy, but only up to the limits specified in the policy and then only for specified perils, such as fire, theft, or windstorm. Unfortunately, most policies provide far from generous coverage on the kinds of items typically stored in a safe-deposit box.

To make sure you have sufficient coverage, you can buy a personal articles "floater" for your homeowner's policy. It will cover any peril, including floods and earthquakes. New items can be insured for their cost; older ones may require a professional appraisal.

Salsa

An excellent red-tomato salsa may be smooth or chunky, mild or hot, spiced with cumin or chili powder (or neither), flavored with lime juice or smoked peppers (or neither), slightly sweet or not sweet at all. Whatever its other traits, it must have a balance of flavors, with the taster able to distinguish among tomatoes, onions, and peppers. It must also taste freshly made.

Salsa is generally a healthy choice for a dip or relish. It has few calories and little to no fat; some brands also have some vitamin C. Only a fresh salsa, though, provides the amount of nutrients found in fresh vegetables. If you are sensitive to sodium, keep in mind that some salsas are quite salty. Check the nutrition label for salt content, and adjust the numbers accordingly if you eat more than the meager serving size listed.

Saws, Saber

Any saber saw needs a comfortable handle and an easy-to-use switch. In the store, try the display samples to see which one fits your hand best. A trigger switch is more convenient than a sliding on-off switch. It's safer, too, because the saw shuts off as soon as your finger lets up on the trigger. A base that can be tilted both right and left lets you set the blade for an angled cut.

As saws move up in price, look for variable cutting speed. Set to run the saw slowly, it permits precise cutting through intricate curves; use a faster speed for straight lines.

Orbital cutting action pulls the blade slightly forward on its upstroke, making it bite aggressively into the material being cut. It helps if you can turn off the orbiting action for fine work. A blade stabilizer—typically, grooved wheels behind the blade or guides clamped on either side—helps prevent the blade from twisting or breaking under stress.

Plunge cuts. You may want to start a cut in the middle of the work—to cut a hole for a light switch in a piece of wall paneling, for example. To make a plunge cut, you tip the saw forward, steady the front edge of the saw's blade on the work, then swing it back slowly until the blade pierces the paneling.

Screwdrivers

A well-equipped workshop might contain a dozen or more screwdrivers, ranging from very small to quite large, with tips to handle slotted screws, Phillips screws, hex-head screws, and more. A minimum complement should be one screwdriver for slotted screws and one for Phillips screws.

The longer and thicker the handle of any screwdriver, the easier it is to use (provided it's not too long for a job that has to be done in close quarters). Avoid handles with sharp corners or rough edges.

Some screwdrivers have a smooth cushioned handle, which is more comfortable than plain hard plastic. But ridged cushioning may be uncomfortable. A handle that's too short or too skinny is hard to hold for long periods and limits the amount of torque you can apply.

The tip on a good slotted screwdriver should have straight, sharp edges. The metal should be free of rough spots or rounded corners.

Some tips have tiny crosswise teeth, a design to keep the tip from slipping out of screw slots. The teeth aren't likely to make a noticeable difference in how easy the tool is to use.

Slotted screwdrivers make natural pry bars. An industry standard says they should be able to withstand a significant amount of bending at the middle of the shaft, with the tip fixed and pressure on the handle. A majority of screwdrivers are likely to meet the standard.

Cordless screwdrivers. Most run on a rechargeable nickel-cadmium battery and resemble a small electric drill or take the form of a hinged stick that can be bent into a pistol shape. They usually have a double-ended bit that has a Phillips tip on one end and a slotted tip on the other. All are reversible, so they can both drive and remove screws. Their shaft can be locked (some lock automatically) and their power turned off, so you can use them like any other screwdriver, twisting them by hand.

Stall torque is the effort that a fully charged screwdriver can apply before it simply stops. The greater the stall torque, the better the screwdriver can tackle demanding jobs.

Most cordless screwdrivers have batteries permanently built into the handle. Some have a removable battery pack. That's an advantage if you work with the tool all the time, since you can buy an extra battery and always have a freshly charged one ready. It also means you don't have to throw away the whole tool when the batteries have been charged and discharged to the point where they are useless.

Cordless screwdriver tips are generally weaker than those on ordinary screwdrivers. Fortunately, replacements are readily available, and they're interchangeable from one brand to another. A useful feature is an adjustable clutch to prevent screws from being driven too far into the work.

Shoes, Dress

Feet are sometimes reluctant to squeeze into dress shoes when they have to walk back to work after a weekend of comfort in athletic shoes. For many people, skinny, stiff leather shoes are out; roomier, gentler shoes are in.

Here are some guidelines to follow when shopping for any shoes:

- Shop late in the day, when your feet are largest. Wear the kind of socks or stockings you plan to wear with the new shoes. If you use orthotics, bring them to the store.

- Try on both right and left shoes; buy for the larger foot. Allow a thumbnail's length of space in front of your longest toe.

- Walk on a hard floor in the store to assess shock absorption.

- Don't buy a shoe that rubs or pinches. Make sure the shoe lets your toes spread out as you walk and that it flexes easily under the ball of the foot.

Shoes, Running

Here are some guidelines to follow when shopping for running shoes:

- Shop late in the day, when your feet are largest.

- Don't expect shoes to stretch.

- Bring an old pair of running shoes to the store—they can help a knowledgeable salesperson analyze the motion of your feet.

- Wear the socks you normally wear for running.

- If you wear orthotic inserts, bring them.

- Check to make sure that the shoes bend easily at their widest point.

- Feel inside for seams and ridges.

- Jog a little in the store (it's worth any embarrassment you may feel).

For a typical running shoe, expect many eyelets, to lace shoes in various ways for a customized fit; uppers of real or synthetic leather and mesh; reflective trim; removable insoles; insoles and midsoles of plastic foam or polyurethane; only D/medium width in men's; only B/medium width in women's. Traction should be at least good on all surfaces. There shouldn't be any heel slippage.

Shopping Channels on TV

If you are a first-time viewer, watch a while before getting caught up in the TV-shopping frenzy. In many cases, the item will be in stock well after it's off the screen, so you can take your time deciding.

Here is other advice for TV shoppers:

- Use a major credit card rather than a personal check. You'll have more leverage if an item isn't what it seemed and the company balks at taking it back.

- Ask for a copy of the company's return policy and money-back guarantee when you order. If the company says it can't oblige, don't order.

- Ignore the suggested retail price.

- Consider having any expensive jewelry item independently appraised once you receive it. An appraisal will generally cost you between $35 and $65.

- With other expensive items, ask the order-taker for the model number and call local retailers for comparison prices. Unless the item is being closed out, it will probably still be available if you call the TV retailer later. Note, however, that some items are exclusive to the TV seller and may not be available in stores.

- Listen closely for size and fit differences on clothing. A misses' size 10 on TV typically runs larger than a 10 at a clothing store. The hosts also will sometimes mention that a particular item fits snugly or loosely or is cut smaller or larger than average.

- Call the company to request a program guide. That could be helpful for finding out when certain types of merchandise will be sold.

Shopping Rights

What if, in the midst of holiday bustle, or at any other time for that matter, you find that you're unhappy with some of your purchases? Or that something you ordered by mail a month ago still hasn't arrived?

Your first step when you're dissatisfied should be to contact the seller or the manufacturer, preferably in writing, so that you'll have a paper trail. But you can head off many kinds of problems in the first place if you plan your shopping strategy with your rights firmly in mind. Those rights vary somewhat from state to state and according to how you make your purchases. Here are some of the basics:

Shopping in person. Unless an item is sold explicitly "as is"—a practice that is illegal in some states—every new product has an "implied warranty" that offers protection if the product doesn't work in ordinary use. Your state's consumer protection office can provide specifics on your state's coverage.

Written warranties come with most major items, although they are not legally required. Such warranties may be "limited," specifying under what circumstances you can have repairs made at no charge, or "full," without limitations. Be sure you understand the extent of the warranty when you buy.

You may or may not get compensation from the seller when you try to return a product simply because you have changed your mind and don't want it anymore. Under the law, a store is not required to exchange or make refunds on items that perform as advertised. Many stores will do so, however, simply as a matter of good public relations.

Shopping by catalog. If you order by mail, you're covered by the Federal Trade Commission's (FTC's) "Mail Order Rule." It specifies that companies must ship an order within the time limit they promise—or if they make no promise, within 50 days. If there is a delay, the company must send a notice with a new shipping date and give you the option of canceling the order.

If the mail-order company can't meet the new date, it must send you another notice. Unless you return a signed consent form at that point, the order will be automatically canceled. If you paid by check or money order, the company must send you a refund within seven business days. If you paid with a charge card, the company must credit your account within one billing cycle.

Some mail-order purchases, such as photofinishing and magazine subscriptions, aren't covered by these laws.

Shopping at home. The FTC's "Cooling Off Rule" specifies that you have three business days to cancel a purchase that cost more than $25 if you made it at your home or at another place that is not the seller's permanent place of business. The seller then has 10 days to refund your money (and return any trade-in that might be involved). The seller also has 20 days to pick up the items or to reimburse you for mailing them back. Some exceptions to the rule: repairs or maintenance on personal property, arts and crafts sold at fairs, and sales made as a result of earlier negotiations at the seller's permanent place of business.

When you buy something in your home, the salesperson is required to provide a cancellation form in case you change your mind. You must send it to the company with a copy of the receipt within the three business days (Saturday counts as a business day) after the purchase. Keep the original receipt and a copy of the cancellation form for yourself.

Shopping with credit. Using a credit card is one of the best safeguards you have against unsatisfactory purchases and uncooperative merchants. Whether you buy in person, by mail order, or by telephone, the Fair Credit Billing Act says that you can withhold payment for unsatisfactory goods or services if all three of the following conditions apply:

1. You can show that you tried to resolve the dispute with the seller.

2. You made the purchase in your home state or within 100 miles of your billing address. For the purpose of establishing where nonstore transactions took place, some states categorize mail-order transactions as originating in the home state. Therefore, if you used your credit card, you'd qualify for protection.

3. You paid more than $50.

There is no specified time period for resolving these disputes. You may withhold payment for the item in question until the matter is resolved, but you must pay the rest of your credit-card bill on schedule.

The Fair Credit Billing Act has a slightly different set of rules for what are classified as "billing errors." First, you must notify the credit-card company in writing, at the address indicated on the bill for "billing errors," within 60 days after the first bill with the error was sent. The card company must acknowledge your letter within 30 days after receiving it, unless the dispute is resolved in the meantime. After that, the law says, the dispute must be resolved within two billing cycles or 90 days, whichever comes first.

Showerheads

During a typical shower, an old showerhead may flow at a rate of three to five gallons per minute (gpm). A new showerhead, by contrast, and in accordance with a federal standard, must put out no more than 2.5 gpm.

A new showerhead can work at least as effectively as an old one and, in addition, is a good investment. (If your household is typical, averaging two four-minute showers a day, you should save enough hot water within two years to pay back the cost of replacing an old showerhead with a moderately priced new one.)

Smoke Detectors

Studies have shown that having a smoke detector in your home cuts your risk of dying in a fire in half. But homes would be safer still if more people took care of their smoke detectors. It's estimated that one in three detectors would not properly respond to a fire, and dead or missing batteries are the leading culprit. Battery-powered smoke detectors are now required to meet a standard: If a detector has no batteries installed, its cover can't be closed or the device must display a visual indicator such as a flag.

Many smoke detectors run on AC power and must be wired into a household circuit. Most such detectors are also equipped with a backup battery. Such dual-power units are required by more and more state and local building codes for newly built residences.

How they work. Smoke detectors that work by ionization are by far the most prevalent kind—some 90 percent of all smoke detectors sold. These units are the fastest type at responding to flaming fires that give off little smoke. Ionization smoke detectors rely on a small amount of radioactive material (so small as to pose no significant health or environmental threat) to make the air between two electrodes conduct a constant electric current. When smoke particles disrupt the current, electronic circuitry sets off the detector's alarm.

Photoelectric smoke detectors are fastest at responding to smoldering, smoky fires. They work by shining a small beam of light past a sensor. When smoke intervenes, it scatters the light into the sensor, activating the alarm.

Features

All smoke detectors have a push button to test whether the unit's electric circuitry, battery, and horn are working correctly. (Almost all detectors also have a small light that flashes periodically to indicate that same state of readiness.) But since detectors are supposed to be mounted high above the floor, those push buttons are often out of easy reach, but may be accessible with a broomstick.

Hush button. Most smoke detectors are hard to quiet once they sound a false alarm (as from cooking smoke). You usually must open a window or detach the detector's battery (and hope you remember to reconnect it later). But a number of models have a hush button that deactivates the alarm for 10 or 15 minutes, before automatically reinstating the alarm to its alert status.

Weak-battery warning. When a detector senses a significant decline in battery voltage, it emits a periodic signal—typically a chirping sound every few minutes—for at least 30 days or until the battery is replaced.

Auxiliary light. A few models turn on built-in reflector lights when the alarm sounds. These are meant to help guide you through smoke. But the lights may be too weak to do the job in a smoky fire; a large halogen-bulb flashlight kept near at hand would be more useful.

Installation. A smoke detector should be installed outside each sleeping area and on each level of your home. A hallway that runs between living spaces and sleeping spaces would be a good site. So would a stairway leading to another level.

You should also install detectors either on the ceiling at least four inches from the nearest wall or high on a wall at least four inches from the ceiling. The reason you shouldn't put a unit too close to an abutting surface is to keep it out of a "dead" air space that might be missed by turbulent hot air bouncing around above a fire.

For similar reasons, a detector shouldn't be set near a window, an exterior door, or anyplace else where drafts might steer smoke away from the unit. Nor should it be installed in areas where you're likely to have false alarms—including the kitchen (because of cooking smoke), the garage (because of car exhaust), and the bathroom (where high humidity can trigger nuisance alarms).

Safety check. Is your detector too old? A detector should work for about 10 years, after which it should be discarded and replaced. Your new detector may come with a reminder label that reads "Replace by 2006." If not, post your own.

Replace a smoke detector's batteries annually with fresh alkaline batteries. Or install nine-volt lithium batteries, which can provide up to six years of service in a smoke detector. Installing rechargeable batteries is not recommended.

Smoking at 65

It's not too late to gain substantial health benefits from quitting smoking at age 65. The earlier a smoker stops, the better; but an extraordinary British study that followed tens of thousands of male doctors for 40 years reported: People who stop before age 35 have the same life expectancy as those who never smoked. Those who stop later in life gain some, but not all, of the non-smokers' life expectancy. If you stop smoking at age 65, you don't collect much of a benefit for a few years; but if you make it to age 75, your chances of dying that year and in each succeeding year will be "appreciably lower" than those who kept on smoking, the researchers said.

Soaps

Today you can buy a product made with synthetic detergent, which will leave less of a bathtub ring than soap does. You can choose a "fragrance-free" soap, an "unscented" soap (which actually contains fragrances to mask the soap smell), or a soap with an exotic fragrance like passion fruit. You can buy a soap to match any decor, in shades from pearly cream to see-through pink to matte black.

Many soapmakers appeal to other senses, promising the likes of "soft feeling, scented skin," or even "energy of body, clarity of mind." But before you believe that you can buy inner or outer beauty in a bar of soap, consider the reality of the claims.

Whereas "boutique" soaps come in nice colors and smells, they won't buy you any more cleanliness than what you'll get with a soap from the supermarket. You can choose any soap with a price and scent you like and be confident that it will clean you. If your skin feels tight after using a product, you're probably washing too frequently—or the soap is working too well, stripping away the skin's natural oils. Try applying a general-purpose moisturizer after washing. If your skin is very sensitive, you may want to try one labeled fragrance-free (not unscented), although you will probably have to pay a little more for it.

Some soaps are more drying than others, but even one that's "one quarter moisturizing cream" will be a poor substitute for a lotion you rub on after bathing. The reason is simple: Much of the moisturizing ingredients in the soap wash off with water, and the rest are likely to towel off when you dry. A brand with aloe vera listed low on the ingredients list isn't likely to contain much of this additive, and is unlikely to leave your hands feeling any better than most other soaps.

Antibacterial soaps have active ingredients to kill germs. Deodorant soaps add a heavier dose of cover-up fragrance. Most deodorant soaps will remove some odor, but so will a dishwashing liquid used in the same way, although some dishwashing liquids may feel a bit harsh on the skin.

Liquid soaps tend to look neater by the sink, but they cost more than bars. In general, a liquid soap works faster than a bar—most likely because it's already in a spreadable form. As an experiment, consider refilling an empty liquid-soap bottle with half dishwashing liquid, half water.

Solvent Hazards

Organic solvents—often petroleum products—are used chiefly to maintain a variety of household products as liquids or pastes or to clean dirt and grease. Most solvents evaporate readily, exposing the user to fumes. The result can be acute, although temporary, intoxication, drowsiness, disorientation, and headache. If fumes are strong enough, the victim may pass out. Many solvents also irritate the eyes and lungs.

Over a longer term of exposure, solvents can affect the nervous system, reproductive system, liver, kidneys, heart, and blood. Some solvents cause cancer in humans and test animals.

People with heart or lung disease and pregnant women should try to avoid products that contain such solvents as methylene chloride and toluene. Other consumers can reduce their exposure (reducing all solvent exposure is generally a good idea) by taking several steps:

- Follow directions. If you're not willing to do that, skip the project altogether or leave it to a professional.

- Consider whether your use of the solvent ingredient is necessary. Often you can substitute a product with little or no solvent for a higher-solvent product. A concrete-type tile cement, for example, can be used instead of a solvent-based adhesive.

- Don't use more than one solvent at a time, and don't use one right after the other.

- Don't drink alcoholic beverages on the day you use solvents; alcohol can heighten their toxic effects. If you take any medicines, ask your doctor about similar interactions.

- Use a fan as you work. Wear a respirator (sold at hardware stores), gloves, and goggles, when called for.

- Note that fumes from some chemicals tend to sink. If you're bent over while working, you may inhale more vapors than when standing.

- Keep solvent products out of children's reach—it's best to lock them up—and keep children out of rooms containing solvent fumes.

Six common organic solvents

Methylene chloride. Found in degreasers, waxes, paints, paint removers, some paint and varnish thinners, pesticide sprays, lubricants.

Effects: The body converts methylene chloride to carbon monoxide and chloride. This solvent affects the heart muscle and heartbeat. Long-term exposure to fumes causes cancer in laboratory animals.

Toluene. Found in gasoline, some glues, some paints, thinners, and paint removers, and some nail polishes.

Effects: Toluene poses risks when inhaled or absorbed through the skin. Low-level exposure affects mental processes and behavior and may affect menstrual functions, hormone levels, and fetal growth and health. Over the long term, exposure affects the liver and heart and can damage the nervous system. Chemically, toluene is related to benzene and xylene, which have similar effects. (Prolonged exposure to benzene is known to cause leukemia and other blood-cell abnormalities.)

1,1,1 trichloroethane. Found in drain cleaners, spot removers, shoe polish, insecticides, printing inks, degreasers.

Effects: Chronic exposure may affect the liver. At high doses, the chemical can also cause damage to the heart and nervous system.

Glycol ethers. Found in antifreeze, some paints, some glues, adhesives, sealants, caulking compounds.

Effects: Poses greatest risk when absorbed through the skin or ingested. Some of these ethers are powerful reproductive poisons that have been shown in animal studies to cause testicular degeneration and malformations in the young born to exposed females. High doses destroy red blood cells and damage the liver. Propylene glycol ethers are less toxic then ethylene glycol ethers.

N-hexane. Found in glues, paints, varnishes, printing inks.

Effects: Few problems result from occasional exposure, but chronic exposure, even at low levels, can severely damage the nervous system.

Petroleum distillates. Found in a wide array of products, including pesticides, paints, paint thinners, furniture polish, adhesives, spot removers, caulking compounds.

Effects: In some painters, a lifetime of exposure has been shown to cause a buildup of fat deposits in the liver. Very high doses can lead to lung problems, anemia, and an irregular heartbeat.

Soups

Canned and dehydrated soups have brought convenience to the kitchen, but something has been lost in the process. As taste tests have shown, many canned soups are so overcooked that if you close your eyes, you probably can't tell whether you are biting into a carrot or a potato.

Without expending too much effort, you can do better by making your own soup, using convenient, readily available, low-cost ingredients and create a soup with appealing flavors and textures.

Homemade chicken soup (recipe follows) has a distinct chicken flavor and firm noodles. Compared with commercial soups it has an average number of calories—105 per eight-ounce serving. The tomato vegetable soup (recipe also follows) will probably taste better to you than any commercial soup you can find.

Chicken noodle soup

Chicken breast half, with skin (about ¾ pound)
¼ cup finely chopped shallots
4 cups water
10½-ounce can condensed chicken broth, reconstituted or 2½ cups ready to serve
½ cup finely diced celery
1¼ teaspoon salt
⅛ teaspoon marjoram
⅛ teaspoon thyme
Pinch black pepper
3 ounces medium-width egg noodles

Place chicken, skin side down, in a preheated 3-quart saucepan. Brown over medium heat long enough to render out some chicken fat (about 5 minutes). Remove chicken. Reduce heat to low. Add shallots and stir briefly (1 to 2 minutes). Do not brown. Return chicken to pan and add remaining ingredients except noodles. Bring to boil. Reduce heat to low simmer and cook 30 minutes or until chicken is tender. Remove chicken. Cool. Discard bones and skin. Dice chicken and return meat to pan. (Soup can be refrigerated for future use at this point.) Just before serving, return soup to boil. Add noodles and cook for required time (about 8 minutes). Yield: about 6½ cups.

Tomato vegetable soup

14½-ounce can diced tomatoes in juice
10½-ounce can condensed chicken broth, reconstituted, or 2½ cups ready to serve
1 cup water
½ cup diced carrots (1 large)
½ cup diced celery (1 rib)
½ cup diced potatoes (1 medium)
½ cup fresh green beans, cut into ½-inch pieces
¼ cup diced onion (1 small)
½ small clove garlic, minced
¼ teaspoon salt
⅛ teaspoon marjoram
⅛ teaspoon thyme
Pinch black pepper

In a 3-quart saucepan, bring tomatoes, broth, and water to a boil. Add vegetables and seasonings. Return to boil. Reduce heat to a slow simmer and cook about 1 hour or until vegetables are tender. Yield: about 5¾ cups.
Vegetarian version: Eliminate chicken broth. Increase water to 3½ cups. Increase salt to ½ teaspoon.

Ramen

Ramen is for people who would rather have a little soup with their noodles than vice versa. It came to this country via Japan, where diners catch the spaghettilike noodles between chopsticks and slurp them from steaming bowls of broth.

Most ramen is sold in plastic-wrapped "pillows" of noodles that come with a packet of dried broth. You toss the noodles and the contents of the packet into boiling water and stir for a few minutes, adding meat or vegetables if you want to. Another type comes in an individual container that serves as a soup bowl. You add boiling water, mix, and eat.

Nutritionally, ramens are slightly worse than other soups. Because their noodles are typically fried before they're dried, ramens are higher in fat and calories. Salt, monosodium glutamate (MSG), and soy sauce in their broth raise their sodium level to between about 800 to 1,000 milligrams per serving, about a third of the recommended daily limit.

Spackling

Before painting indoors, repair damaged surfaces, smooth over chipped paint, and fill in holes, scratches, tears, and dents. Modern spackling compounds are preferred over patching plasters or plaster of paris.

Types. Powders mixed with water resist cracking and shrinking quite well, and create a strong patch. Regular premixed pastes are convenient, but most tend to shrink and crack as they dry. Lightweight pastes, a mixture of spackling and tiny glass spheres, resist cracking and shrinking but don't make a very strong patch and may take extra coats of paint to get a uniform luster.

Steam Irons

Extra features make the modern steam iron more convenient than ever. Some irons are helped along by a burst of steam when you press a button. Irons usually let you push a button to spray ahead as you go. That helps when you iron challenging fabrics like linen, set creases, and do general spot dampening.

Irons typically let you turn off the steam so you can dry-iron. That's useful when you set the temperature low for delicate items; if you left the steam on and the temperature wasn't high enough to turn the water into steam, you'd get streaks of water on delicate fabrics. Most irons have an easy-to-clean nonstick soleplate coating.

Automatic shutoff, a safety feature, can save you the headache of making a trip back home for fear you might have left the iron on. But even with automatic shutoff, it's a good idea to make sure the iron is turned off and unplugged before you leave the ironing board. Most irons switch themselves off after about one-half minute lying flat—fast enough to avoid damage—and from 8 to 15 minutes standing upright. Moving the iron usually starts it heating again.

Stir-Frying

Stir-frying can be a healthful, low-fat cooking method, but many people defeat the purpose by pouring on oil as they cook. To stir-fry properly, begin with a small amount of oil and add only water or broth if foods become dry during cooking.

Stolen Check Liability

What happens if your checkbook is stolen, a number of checks forged, and your bank refuses to credit your account for the amount of the checks? The law varies from state to state. In most states, banks are liable if they pay a check that the customer did not sign. However, a bank may refuse to reimburse you if it believes you were negligent. Negligence may include failing to safeguard your checks, filling them out in a way that made them easy to alter, or failing to notify the bank about the loss in a timely manner. Your state's banking department may be able to mediate with the bank on your behalf.

Strep Infection, Children

It can be trying and costly to take one or more children to the doctor every time they get sore throats, for fear of strep infections and the possible complications. However, concerns about strep are valid. In a small minority of cases, untreated streptococcal infections can cause rheumatic fever or kidney disease. Treatment with antibiotics can prevent these complications. But only a throat culture can tell whether a sore throat is caused by strep and therefore requires antibiotic therapy.

Nevertheless, it's possible to lower medical bills in some circumstances. If a child has sniffles and a cough as well as a sore throat, then it's unlikely to be strep; a phone call to the doctor may be all you need. On the other hand, if more than one child is sick at the same time with sore throats, fever, and lymph-node enlargement—the typical signs of strep throat—and if one of them has a positive strep culture, then it's reasonable to assume that other children in the family are probably also infected. In that case, all can be treated with antibiotics simultaneously. (There is no reason for a doctor to give antibiotics as a preventive measure to family members who have no symptoms of strep.)

It's a good idea to ask the doctor whether he or she can take a throat culture without charging for a full office visit. Some doctors may be willing to do this if a full exam may be unnecessary.

Strollers

If you're buying for a newborn, a convertible carriage/stroller makes the most sense because you can use it first as a carriage and later, when the baby can sit up, as a stroller. Convertible strollers also tend to be fairly comfortable and durable, and easy to handle. The seatback reclines enough to let the baby sleep in the stroller. Then by raising the seatback and flipping the handle, you can convert the carriage to a stroller. Lightweight strollers fold up to a tidy package that can be carried like a big furled umbrella.

Tandem and side-by-side models are for parents with two stroller-age children. Tandems, which put one child behind the other, appeal because they are easy to maneuver in tight quarters.

Jogging strollers, designed so the runner in the family can take the baby along, have three bicycle-type wheels, making them easy to push over uneven ground. Car seat/stroller combinations let you move between sidewalk and car without lifting the baby from the seat.

Safety. There is a voluntary industry safety standard for strollers. Nevertheless, look for the following shortcomings:

- Movable parts capable of injuring a baby, plus parts small enough to be swallowed or inhaled.

- Brakes that don't hold on a slope.

- No effective backup safety latches to prevent the stroller from accidentally collapsing.

- Safety belts that don't provide enough restraint.

- A stroller that tends to tip backward with relatively little pressure on the handles, even when carrying the weight of baby.

Look for the following convenience features on any stroller:

- Adequate padding over metal parts, shock absorption to

cushion the bumps, and a wide seat that's deep enough for a large baby.

- A backrest with a rigid insert for good support.

- Padding that's easy to clean. Not all fabrics are machine-washable and not all pads are removable.

- Any stroller should be easy to open and fold, ideally with one hand.

- The stroller should be easy to steer and push, whether the person handling it is short or tall. Test-drive it to be sure it can go straight without veering when you use one hand.

- Generally, the larger the wheels, the more easily the stroller will handle curbs and uneven terrain. Strollers easiest to maneuver have swivel wheels and locks to stop the front wheels from veering on soft ground.

Sulfites in Wine

Why do wine bottle labels include the words "contains sulfites"? Some people—most of them asthmatics—are allergic to sulfite compounds, which have long been used as preservatives in wines. Federal regulations have required this labeling since 1987.

Sunscreens

Skin cancer is "epidemic," dermatologists say, with 700,000 or more new cases per year in the United States. And perhaps 90 percent of those cancers are linked to overexposure to the sun.

As the sun's hazards have become clear, many Americans have taken cover, buying more sunscreen and upgrading to more protective products. Over the past 10 years, the norm has escalated from sunscreens with a sun-protection factor (SPF) of 4 or lower—which lets users tan or, if they're careless, burn—to SPF 15 or higher, which allows most people a few hours of sunbathing, sailing, or sports with no tan or burn at all. Although sunscreen products are available with higher SPF factors, SPF 15 to 18 is the protection level recommended for general use by dermatologists, cancer experts, and public health officials.

Be sure to use enough sunscreen. Consider "enough" to be one ounce, a generous handful, to cover those parts of an adult's body not covered by a bathing suit. Since most sunscreens come in four-ounce containers, that's one-quarter of the contents.

Sunscreens work best when applied half an hour before going out. Some, especially those with zinc and titanium oxides, must be shaken well; those particles can settle or clump in a lotion, and they must be spread uniformly to achieve the best protection.

If you want to tan, you could try an SPF 2 to 8, start out with short exposures, and carefully increase your time outdoors over several days, to let your skin build up melanin (the dark pigment that the body produces in response to sunlight). But most medical authorities recommend against it. The tan itself is your body's protective response to the sun's damage. If you get a tan, you're needlessly aging your skin and increasing your risk of skin cancer.

Some sunscreens are better than others at staying on your skin when you get wet, but you generally pay extra for long-term waterproofing.

Sunscreens and vitamin D. Sunscreens block solar radiation responsible for producing vitamin D in the skin. But for most people, it takes only a few minutes of morning or late afternoon sun on the face, hands, and lower arms, two or three days a week during the spring and summer to provide the body with many months worth of vitamin D. People who are housebound should make sure they get about 400 units of vitamin D daily from diet or supplements.

Surge Suppressors for Computers

Surge suppressors guard against equipment damage by providing an alternate pathway for electrical energy when excessive voltage suddenly appears on the power line. Suppressors contain components that electrically absorb the energy, shunting it away from vulnerable computer circuits.

Nearby lightning strikes can cause current surges, or "spikes," and the electrical wiring in your home can act as a channel for the disturbance. Line surges can also originate with the utility company. Very low indoor humidity can generate potentially damaging static electricity.

A surge suppressor represents a sensible form of insurance, even for a computer with a degree of built-in surge protection. You should consider only models with a statement on the package that they meet the Underwriter Laboratories (UL) standard 1449 for TVSS. The UL listing should include three ratings, one for each pairing of line, neutral, and ground wires. The lowest and best UL 1449 rating is 330 volts (.33 kV), the average voltage the device is supposed to allow through. Steer clear of devices with a rating higher than 500 volts—that's unnecessarily high.

Don't limit the use of a surge suppressor to the computer itself. Be sure all peripheral equipment—printers, fax machines, modems, and the like—are also connected.

Sweaters

Sweater warmth. A sweater's ability to "breathe" affects warmth. As a woven fabric (like shirting), cotton breathes well. But in sweaters, cotton yarns lend themselves to tight knitting, making relatively heavy sweaters that absorb perspiration. Fluffy acrylic yarns make a less dense knit that's better able to let perspiration escape. Thus, you feel dry and therefore warmer.

Wool fibers make fluffy yarns, too, but absorb perspiration more than acrylic yarns.

Bulky sweaters—whether made from a thick, fuzzy acrylic or a heavy, sturdy wool—always look warmer than thin ones. Usually, they are.

Weight isn't a reliable indicator of warmth unless you're comparing two sweaters of similar knit made of the same fiber—then the heavier sweater will be thicker and therefore warmer. Weight comparisons don't work if the sweaters are different styles. A loose-fitting sweater, such as a tunic style, made of a simple, flat knit could weigh more than a close-fitting sweater knitted from bulky yarns. But the latter is likely to be warmer. A thin cotton sweater will weigh a lot more than a thin cashmere, but the cashmere will usually be warmer.

Swimmer's Ear

To prevent the infection known as "swimmer's ear," don't let water stay trapped after showering or swimming. Here's one way to dry a stubborn ear, suggested by the American Academy of Otolaryngology: Tip your head over with the wet ear up, pull the ear up and back, and empty a medicine dropper of rubbing alcohol into the ear canal; wiggle or pull your ear to coax the drops all the way in, and then turn your head to the other side to let the ear drain.

Tampons and Feminine Hygiene Pads

Even the most absorbent feminine hygiene pad is a poor choice if it doesn't fit comfortably. Getting a good fit may simply mean attaching the pad in the right place, or it may mean trying different pads.

A tampon should be so comfortable that you aren't aware of it. If you can feel it, insert the next one at a slightly different angle or depth, or try another brand. If you're afraid to try a new tampon for fear that an ill fit will cause an accident, try using a feminine hygiene pad for extra protection while you experiment.

If your tampon:

- Feels too long, try a product that doesn't expand lengthwise.

- Irritates when you remove it, try a less-absorbent tampon or use a pad.

- Resists when you insert it, try a tampon with a narrower applicator.

- Pokes as you insert it, check to see that the petals aren't misshapen.

If your pad:

- Doesn't stay in place, try a pad with wings.

- Irritates the inside of your thighs, try a pad without wings or side gathers.

- Bunches and gets out of shape, try a pad that's narrower, or one with an hourglass shape.

- Doesn't provide enough coverage, try a pad that's wider or longer.

- Doesn't feel soft enough, try a product with a clothlike feel.

Tape Decks

The most widely available decks are component-size units, either single-deck or dual-deck machines. (However, for recording enthusiasts, there are expensive minidisc recorders that offer the sound quality and all the playback advantages of a CD player.)

Buying advice. Choose a dual deck if you want hours of uninterrupted background music or if you frequently copy tapes. If you do a lot of serious recording, you're probably better off with a single deck, which should give you more flexibility during the recording process. In the store, make sure a deck's controls, functions, and features are easy to use.

Teeth, Gum Disease

Several factors can raise the risk of gum disease. If any of these apply, take especially good care of your mouth—and make sure your dentist or periodontist examines your gums carefully.

- *Pregnancy or birth-control pills.* Hormonal changes can make gums sensitive and more vulnerable to bacteria.

- *Smoking.* Tobacco smoke irritates oral tissue, increases tartar and the risk of new gum disease, and impedes healing after gum treatment.

- *Alcohol.* Drinks tend to dry saliva, which would normally slow plaque buildup.

- *Medications.* Some decongestants, muscle relaxants, tranquilizers, antidepressants, antihistamines, antihypertensives, and antispasmodics cut the flow of saliva. Others, such as calcium-channel blockers, stimulate gum tissue overgrowth.

- *Impaired immunity.* Diabetes and AIDs both impair resistance, which plays a role in gum disease.

- *Family history of juvenile gum disease.* Young people whose relatives have had gum disease should be examined at least annually.

Teeth, Preventing Decay

Fluoridated water and toothpaste have drastically reduced tooth decay in children. Plastic dental sealants could prevent virtually all of the remaining cavities, but only one child in 10 has had sealants applied. For best results, the dentist should apply sealant to the biting surfaces of permanent molars soon after they erupt.

Teeth, Sensitivity

The problem most people experience with sensitive teeth is caused when receding gums and vigorous brushing expose and wear down the neck of the tooth, the junction between the crown and root. This makes it easier for sensations of physical contact or cold to be transmitted to the local nerve endings.

Dentists recommend three levels of treatment. The first is to brush with a desensitizing toothpaste, which contains compounds that help block transmission of sensation from the tooth to the nerve. There are two active ingredients on the market that work in different ways: strontium chloride and potassium nitrate. If one doesn't work, try the other.

The second level is for your dentist to prescribe a stannous fluoride gel that you can apply to sensitive teeth. The gel can bind to the tooth and reduce the transmission of sensation through it.

Finally, if that doesn't work, your dentist can seal the sensitive area with plastics or cements. Sometimes these are inserted like fillings; sometimes they are painted onto the tooth's surface.

Telephone Answering Machines

Telephone answering machines used to do little more than record reliably and play back messages intelligibly. Now, some full-feature machines can:

- Keep messages for several family members in separate "mailboxes," each mailbox having its own greeting and access code.

- Call you at another location to let you know you've just received a message, and then play the message.

- Answer calls from two different phone lines in one home.

- Let you call in and monitor the room the answering machine is in.

- Use a synthesized voice to stamp calls with their date and time.

- Let you leave a voice memo for another family member, who can then retrieve your memo as though it were a phone message.

Machines are also smaller, more efficient, and more reliable than they used to be. Almost gone from the market are bulky, trouble-prone machines with two tape cassettes—one to carry the owner's greeting, the other to record incoming messages. If answering machines use tape at all now, it's usually in a single microcassette that only records messages. The trend is to use computer chips, which can record many more minutes of messages than they did in the first machines, to employ "tapeless" recording.

Answering machines have also changed through their integration with the telephone. If you're in the market for both an answering machine and a telephone, many integrated machines are less expensive (and most are less bulky) than a separate phone and answering machine.

An alternative. A popular alternative to the home answering machine is to pay the telephone company to record your missed calls on a digital voice-mail system. You dial into the system and receive your messages, record new greetings, and so on. Monthly costs typically range from about $3 for basic answering to $7 and up for service with such features as multiple mailboxes. Voice mail is generally more reliable and more immune to power outages than a typical home answering machine, and it requires no upfront investment. However, given that answering machines are becoming cheaper to buy, it will probably be more expensive in the long run to subscribe to voice mail than to own an answering machine.

Telephone Rates

The phone industry has created a tangle of rates, plans, and incentives ensuring that some consumers pay more than others for the same long-distance calls. It's smart to review your calling pattern and pick a suitable discount calling plan. Even if you spend less than $10 a month, you can benefit from plan membership, and the savings usually rise in step with monthly spending.

It's at least worth checking with AT&T (800-222-0300), MCI (800-444-3333), and Sprint (800-746-3767) to get comparative price information about the cheapest plan for you. If you decide to change, the new company will usually pick up the tab local telephone companies charge to switch your long-distance service.

Check back about once a year: New plans and incentives are added steadily, and you can't rely on your company to alert you to them.

Television Sets

TV sets are defined by screen size: pocket-size (3- to 4-inch LCD screen); small (5- to 13-inch screen); medium (19- or 20-inch screen); large (25- to 40-inch screen); and projection sets (41 inches and up). TV/VCR combinations are also available (see TV/VCR Combinations). Most sets provide good picture quality when fed a clean, strong signal.

The amount of detail that many TV sets display is close to the best possible with the broadcast-signal format used in the United States. (High-definition TV—HDTV—will be the next major improvement, but HDTV won't be in common use for at least several years—and it will be very expensive initially.) And brightness and contrast are usually sufficient to give pictures "punch." People who watch cable may sometimes see slight increases in picture "noise" or faint fluctuations in brightness because the adjacent channel's signal is interfering with the signal of the channel being watched.

Sound quality is more variable than picture quality. Medium-size sets typically sound no better than a mediocre boombox. Larger stereo TV sets tend to deliver better sound, but even their fidelity falls short of what you would hear with a good audio system, especially in the bass. To take full advantage of stereo broadcasts, you have to connect external speakers, usually through a hi-fi.

Thermostats, Energy-Saving

You can save energy and money in the winter by turning down the thermostat. The saving can be substantial: In the upper Midwest, for example, setting back the temperature from 68°F to 55°F at night can save at least $10 to $20 a month on fuel. You'll achieve such savings with any thermostat—if you remember to set and reset it daily. Or, you can use an automatic setback thermostat. A setback thermostat offers comfort and convenience, since it can turn the heat on before you get out of bed or raise the temperature before you come home in the evening. A setback thermostat also offers dependability, since it will automatically change the temperature day in and day out.

There are two basic types of setback thermostats. Digital electronic models offer the greatest number of temperature settings and setback periods, but they can be quite complex to program. Electromechanical thermostats are easier to set but have fewer features and offer less flexibility.

Time-Share Real Estate

Instead of buying a vacation home, you might be tempted to buy a week or two at a time-share resort. A time-share entitles you to the use of a unit for a week or more each year. As of September 1994, the average week cost $7,800 to buy, with an annual maintenance fee of $316. Buyers can generally swap their shares for a visit to another time-share location.

Buy a time-share only if you expect to use it, bearing in mind:

- A time-share is not an investment. Most of them fall in value.

- If you want to buy a time-share, look for a unit for sale by its owner; it will probably be much less expensive than a comparable new unit.

- A time-share may not be easy to exchange. If you want to make exchanges, buy a desirable week in a desirable place and try to plan your vacation very early.

Toaster Oven-Broilers

Toasters take up less room than a toaster oven-broiler and make better toast, faster and easier. But people with limited counter space often go for a toaster oven or broiler because it can handle extra chores—typically heating breads and pastries, reheating pizza slices, or cooking burgers (and rolls) for lunch. During broiling, the bottom elements are generally off and the top ones are operating at full power, with the food close to the heat. *What to look for.* The toasting rack should be removable and should advance an inch or so when the door is opened. The rack height should be adjustable, so you can move it closer to the heating element for broiling and farther from it for baking. Extra overhead clearance lets you fit bulky items.

Most oven pans are aluminum; ones made of steel or coated with porcelain are sturdier. For broiling, food goes on a metal grid that fits into the pan. Grease drips through slits in the grid onto the pan, shielding it from the heat to inhibit smoking.

Look for a removable crumb tray. A hinged bottom is somewhat less convenient. And no crumb tray at all (you turn the appliance upside down and shake it) is downright inconvenient. A removable door is handy for cleaning. A continuous-clean surface mostly hides stains and can't withstand scouring.

Toasters

In recent years, manufacturers have introduced several key design changes, notably an all-plastic housing that stays cool to the touch and a single, elongated slot that's wide enough to accept thick slices. Compared with old-fashioned models, which have openings as small as ¾ inch, a typical wide-mouth toaster's slot typically measures 1⅛ inches. Some slots are as wide as 1⅜ inches—enough clearance for even the largest cut bagel. But be careful: Some models labeled "wide slot" have slots only as wide as a standard toaster's.

For easiest cleaning, look for a removable tray in the base. Second best is a hinged door. Worst is nothing at all: You have to turn the toaster upside down and shake out the crumbs.

Single-slot toasters generally do a better job than models with two side-by-side slots.

Toilet Tank, Water Savings

Try retrofitting an old water-wasting toilet instead of buying a low-flow model: Put a sand-filled soda bottle in the tank. That can save as much as a gallon of water with each flush.

Water leaks from the overflow tube. Sprinkle a little talcum powder on the water in the tank. If the powder moves toward the

overflow tube, water is being lost. Sometimes the float arm can be bent to shut off the valve before water spills into the overflow.
Leaks from the flush valve or flapper. When water leaks into the bowl at this point, the water level in the tank goes down and then refills; the toilet sounds as if it's flushing when no one is using it. Try lengthening the chain connecting the valve with the flush lever by a link or two. If the leak persists, replace the flapper (available in home supply stores).
Buy a new toilet? A federal standard for water consumption of new toilets imposes a limit of 1.6 gallons per flush. Whereas a new toilet will use less water than an old one, only people who pay exorbitant water and sewer rates should buy a commode primarily as a way to save money. Assuming average water costs, even an inexpensive new toilet will take about a decade to pay for itself through lower bills.

Tomatoes

When shopping for tomatoes during the summer, look for backyard, farmstand, or other local tomatoes—they'll almost always taste better than those you can buy elsewhere. During the winter, consider buying cherry tomatoes instead, and plum tomatoes for cooking. To maximize the flavor of any unripe tomatoes, store them in a paper bag at room temperature; never refrigerate them.

Toys and Games

When buying toys, here are some tips to keep in mind.

Consider toys that relate to the child's age, interests, and abilities—not yours.

It is wrong to assume that the bigger and costlier a toy, the greater its play value. Simple, inexpensive toys such as building blocks, crayons, and crafts lend themselves to creative play. Similarly, pots, pans, boxes, and other household items entertain at length because children are free to make of them what they like: musical instruments, race cars, or forts.

Examine the toy closely. If possible, open the package to look at all the parts. Check the box or individual parts for safety warnings. If you are buying a toy for an infant or toddler, make sure all seams and small parts are secure.

Look for sturdy construction. Toys that appear flimsy probably are. If a child is rough on toys, pass up models that look as though they won't stand the abuse.

Examine assembly instructions. If the job seems too involved, ask whether the store will do it.

Games. Traditional types of games have not only survived but thrived in the face of the onslaught of their video counterparts. Unlike video games, which can entertain only one or two people at a time, traditional games bring groups of friends or family members together. They also bring the generations together. A number of games that are top sellers today were around more than 30 years ago, so parents, grandparents, uncles, and aunts don't have to learn any new rules in order to play. Traditional games also tend to be cheaper—much cheaper—than video games.

Trash Compactors

A compactor can be used either freestanding or under the kitchen counter. In use, the compactor's door is pulled out and garbage is loaded into a disposable bag that's designed to fit the bin. An electric motor, activated by a key lock, drives a flat steel ram downward to crush the trash. The bag is usually secured by retainer buttons on the bin. To remove the bag, a latch is released and (on most models) the bag is lifted out in a caddy.

Safety problems with home trash compactors are a rarity. Interlocks prevent the door from being opened during a cycle and prevent the compactor from operating when the bin and door are not properly closed. All models have key locks that prevent children from operating the machine (although the compactor door does not lock when the machine is idle).

Whereas compressed trash may reduce landfill needs slightly, the home trash compactor offers few or no environmental advantages. For many households, buying one offers little except the opportunity to carry fewer, if heavier, loads of trash, to the curb or the dump. However, for those with pay-as-you-throw garbage billing, a compactor may pay for itself in fairly short order.

Treasury Securities

Many people are attracted to U.S. Treasury securities because of their safety and also because their interest income is exempt from state and local taxes.

Treasury securities come in three basic varieties: *Treasury bills* are short-term obligations, issued in three-, six-, and 12-month maturities. *Treasury notes* are issued in two-, three-, five-, and 10-year maturities. *Treasury bonds* are long-term obligations, issued in 30-year maturities.

Zero-coupon bonds. These bonds are issued at sharp discounts from their face value. Instead of paying out interest in cash every six months, as conventional bonds do, zeros pay "phantom" interest. You never get your hands on the money, but you must pay taxes on it unless you hold the securities in a tax-deferred account, such as an IRA. The cumulative value of that interest is reflected in what you receive when you redeem the zeros for their full face value at maturity. Treasury zeros are popular with parents trying to build a college fund or for people planning retirement.

Tuna Canned in Oil

Tuna is a good source of omega-3 fatty acids, a beneficial kind of fish oil. But don't expect to get an extra dose of fish oil with a can of tuna packed in vegetable oil. Tuna packed in water is just as high in omega-3 fatty acids—but much lower in fat and calories. (Canned salmon, on the other hand, often comes packed in salmon oil, which is quite high in desirable omega-3 fatty acids.)

Turkey

To prevent any bacteria from spreading while handling turkey, keep your hands clean and use hot soapy water to wash the cutting board, knives, sink, and anything else that touches the raw meat. Refrigeration at 40°F or below slows the growth of bacteria; cooking to high temperatures (165°F to 212°F) kills bacteria. The goal should be to keep the turkey out of that dangerous middle zone.

A frozen turkey should stay in the freezer until you're ready to thaw it. A fresh one should be kept in the refrigerator and used within a day or two of purchase. Keep turkey in its original wrapping until you're ready to prepare it for cooking.

Thawing a frozen turkey. First, two don'ts: Don't leave a frozen turkey out to thaw on the counter. Don't thaw a prestuffed frozen turkey before you cook it. Instead, use the following methods.

- The simplest way to thaw an unstuffed bird is in the refrigerator, which takes about one day for every five pounds. Put the bird in a pan or tray so the juices won't drip down onto other foods.

- A faster way is to place the wrapped turkey in the sink and cover it with cold water. It will take about half an hour per pound to thaw, and you should change the water every half hour or so.

• Finally, you can thaw the turkey in a microwave oven, following instructions for the size bird the oven will hold, the minutes per pound, and the power level needed for thawing.

After the turkey has thawed, reach in and take out the neck and giblets. Thoroughly wash the inside and outside with cold water, drain, and pat dry with paper towels.

Stuffing the stuffing. There are advantages to cooking the stuffing separately: The turkey will roast faster; the stuffing can be lighter because it won't absorb any turkey fat; and it can't be contaminated by the turkey.

But stuffing cooked in the bird is likely to be moister and tastier. Put the stuffing in the turkey just before it goes into the oven, packing it loosely so it will heat to a safe temperature. When the turkey is cooked, take the stuffing out immediately. Don't stuff a turkey you plan to microwave.

Roasting. You can cook the bird in an open roasting pan or you can roast it in a covered pan, in a pan topped loosely with a foil tent, or in a cooking bag inside a pan. Whatever your style, set the oven to no lower than 325°F and insert a meat thermometer into the thickest part of the inner thigh muscle without touching the bone. The bird is done when the thigh temperature reaches 180°F to 185°F, the drumstick is soft and moves easily at the joint, and the juices run clear.

Pop-up timers sometimes pop up prematurely, and some may not pop up at all. A thermometer is more reliable.

After cooking. After removing the stuffing, let the meat sit for about 20 minutes to make carving easier. Refrigerate or freeze any leftovers within two hours of taking the turkey from the oven. Divide what's left into small portions that can cool quickly. Cut the meat from the bone before wrapping or it will dry out. Finish refrigerated stuffing and gravy in two days, turkey in four.

TV/VCR Combinations

Because the combination of a television set and a VCR housed in the same cabinet uses a single chassis and tuner for both components, you can make the combo work simply by connecting the antenna cable and plugging in the power cord. But the single tuner limits flexibility. You can't watch one TV program while taping another, a capability most VCR owners take for granted.

Although a TV/VCR may deliver a respectable TV picture and can record and play tapes capably, its lack of features makes it more suitable as a household's second or third set, or as an all-in-one unit for a college dorm room.

V

··

Vacation Money

From a safety perspective, it makes sense to carry more money in the form of traveler's checks than to carry cash or personal checks and to take along a credit card or two when vacationing. (See Stolen Check Liability.) Your liability for stolen credit cards is usually $50 or less; stolen traveler's checks are generally reimbursed in full.

You can save a few dollars if you know where to buy traveler's checks. American Express charges $1 for every $100 worth of its traveler's checks, whereas many local American Automobile Association (AAA) offices offer the same traveler's checks free of additional charge to their members. Some banks and credit cards also offer free traveler's checks.

Using ATMs. Look for an automatic teller machine (ATM) that displays the logo of the card you're using (MasterCard or Visa, for example). But be aware that using your credit card to get cash can be costly. You'll usually pay a fee of 1–3 percent of the total amount. And if your card lacks a grace period for cash advances, you will start to pay interest from the moment you take money from the ATM machine.

You may also be able to use your bank ATM card instead of a credit card, as long as the card and the ATM share a common computer network logo (Cirrus, Star, or PLUS, for example). Funds from such ATM transactions come directly from your bank account.

When spending money abroad, you have to look at the rate

of exchange as well as the cost of whatever you're purchasing. You'll generally get the best rate if you charge purchases directly to your credit card. If you pay your credit-card bill in full every month and have a card with an interest-free grace period, you'll also be getting a no-interest loan from the time you make your purchase until you pay your bill.

Generally, the worst conversion rates and highest fees are at airports and other locations where you can't shop for a better deal. Hotels and shops are convenient places to change money but can easily cost 10–15 percent more than banks and other financial institutions.

When you change money, also beware of any transaction fees. It pays to estimate your cash needs beforehand and make a minimum number of exchanges: A fee of $5 or $10 per transaction is expensive if you're changing $50 once or twice a day. *Coming home.* Chances are, you'll do better on the exchange rate if you convert foreign currency while still abroad.

Try to bring only paper money back to the United States. Foreign coins usually cannot be exchanged. With some of them worth $1.50 or more, a pocketful of coins can be an expensive souvenir.

Travel insurance. For most people, trip-cancellation insurance is the only kind of policy worth buying. It reimburses you if you have to cancel or interrupt a trip and would lose a substantial prepayment. It may make sense if, for example, work demands or health problems could upset your travel plans.

For other risks, such as stolen luggage or a medical emergency, see what coverage your existing insurance already provides. Check your homeowner's or renter's insurance policy for personal property coverage away from home. Your health insurance may already provide for medical emergencies overseas. And many credit cards offer accident insurance when you use them to purchase tickets from airlines, tour operators, or cruise lines.

Vacations, Planning

The fourth quarter of the year—up to the beginning of the Christmas through the New Year's holiday period—is low season in many of the world's primary vacation areas. The summer peak ends sometime around Labor Day, and the winter season doesn't really begin until the weekend before Christmas. Although business travel keeps hotels in the world's major cities humming through much of the autumn, the period between Thanksgiving and Christmas is often a dead season for business travel, too, and thus for big-city hotels.

Accordingly, you're likely to be able to find attractive off-season rates for October, November, and December in resort areas active mainly in peak summer season; in Caribbean beach centers that target travelers seeking relief from winter storms; in winter sports centers, where the snow and ice don't occur until December or January; and from cruise lines. By early September, you'll start spotting specific offers in the travel sections of your Sunday papers or at travel agencies.

If you can travel off-season, you'll save a lot on accommodations. But you won't have the experience that you'd have at the same place during its busy season. A Caribbean beach in October, when the weather is still pleasant back home, doesn't really offer the same relief that it does when your home temperature is 10° below and your driveway is under five feet of snow. (You may even find the air temperature a bit chilly for swimming.) By the same token, Aspen, Vail, and Breckenridge in late autumn aren't the same when it's too early to ski and too late for summer festivals.

Travelers who want to take advantage of off-season rates should choose their locations with some care. If possible, find a spot where autumn weather will be comfortable and where you can still find whatever mix of outdoor and indoor recreation and entertainment you prefer.

Vacuum Cleaners

An upright vacuum is best for most homes. As a rule, one will be less expensive than a canister vacuum and easier to move around and store. Canisters are best suited to homes with more bare floors than rugs or carpeting.

A good vacuum cleaner should be able to pull dirt from deep within carpet pile. Upright models used to excel, but now there's little difference between a good canister and a good upright.

Any cleaner should be as easy to use as possible. Here are some factors to consider:

- You can usually lift an upright with one hand. Canisters typically require two hands.

- Deep cleaning goes better when the beater brushes are adjusted to the right height. Most reliable are adjustments you can make yourself, rather than the automatic kind.

- Most uprights—especially those with big wheels or rollers—are not difficult to push when the beater brushes are set at the right height. Self-propulsion takes some getting used to. Uprights require more effort to move about when the hose is in use than when they're deep cleaning. A few have hoses that are mounted high on the machine, making the vacuum prone to tip.

- On stairways, a canister vacuum is generally easier to use than an upright.

- The power nozzle of a canister vacuum usually fits more readily under furniture than the bulkier power head of an upright.

How much power? Claims of amperage, peak horsepower, and "cleaning effectiveness per amp" adorn vacuum cleaners, but there's no correlation between the claims and cleaning performance.

Light vacuums. A lightweight, compact "stick" vacuum cleaner (also called an electric broom) can be handy for quick once-overs on floors in, say, the kitchen or a small apartment. It may also be a boon for someone with limited mobility or hand strength who has trouble using either a full-size vacuum cleaner or a broom and dustpan.

Variable Annuities

It may be tempting to listen to a bank's sales pitch for a variable annuity in place of a renewed CD, but there are some pitfalls to such a trade.

Variable annuities are insurance products that involve investments, such as stocks, bonds, or money-market funds. You won't owe tax on any investment gains until you withdraw the money after age 59½, but if you need it before that, you'll have to pay a substantial early-withdrawal penalty. Variable annuities also have high annual fees. In addition, unlike a bank CD, your investment isn't federally insured, and the rate of return is not guaranteed.

Vegetable Nutrition

The "fresh" vegetables available in supermarkets and greengrocers have usually been hauled across the country and displayed for a few days. That leaves plenty of time for air, heat, and light to break down vitamins. Frozen vegetables are especially likely to be better than fresh vegetables that are out of season or that sit in the refrigerator for more than a couple of days. For maximum nutrition, don't thaw frozen vegetables before cooking. (Vegetables clumped together in the bag indicate thawing somewhere along the line.)

Canned vegetables don't stack up to fresh or frozen vegetables. Much of the vitamin content (not to mention taste) is destroyed by high processing temperatures or lost to water in the can.

Videocassette Recorders

Most videocassette recorders (VCRs) are VHS models, in either hi-fi stereo or monophonic versions. If hi-fi sound is not important to you, a monophonic VCR will save you money. However, if you do want high-quality sound, a hi-fi VCR is worth the extra $50 or more. But the better sound is achievable only with good speakers.

"High-band" formats—S-VHS and Hi8—boast special effects, editing features, and excellent picture quality, but they require expensive tapes and a TV set good enough to show off all their abilities. Most manufacturers offer at least some models with VCR Plus, which can simplify recording television programs. VCR Plus should be able to control a cable box if you want to record scrambled programs.

There's no clear relationship between price and picture quality. As a rule, though, more money buys more convenience and more features. Look for a tuner that receives 125 cable channels; ability to record at SP and EP speeds and play tapes recorded at SP, LP, and EP; on-screen setup and programming of eight events up to 30 days in advance, with options for daily and weekly recording; power that turns on when tape is inserted; auto rewind at end of tape; automatic head cleaning; four video heads that produce noise-free slow motion and frame advance; a counter that counts in hours/minutes/seconds. Other noteworthy features include jog-shuttle, which helps you maneuver through a tape, and go-to and index search, which help you locate specific scenes.

Videotape

VHS cassettes are used in VCRs and in some camcorders. Most compact camcorders use regular VHS-C or 8mm cassettes. The "high-band" tapes (S-VHS-C and Hi8) used in expensive camcorders are designed to yield a somewhat sharper picture. Standard T120 VHS tape, used in VCRs and a few camcorders, holds two hours of material at the machine's fastest speed, as does an 8mm tape. Standard VHS-C tape holds 30 minutes at the fastest speed. Longer lengths of VHS and VHS-C tapes are available, as are different "grades."

However, there's negligible correlation between price and performance. For most normal recording, you can buy by price, not by grade or brand. You may want to choose a tape designated as "high-grade" for recording a special event, however.

Follow these steps to protect the videotapes you care most about:

• To prevent loss from fire or other catastrophes, make a copy and store it away from the original.

• After copying, to prevent accidental erasure, remove the tab on the spine of the videocassette.

• To seal a videocassette from smoke, dust, and dirt, enclose it in a plastic box, the sturdier the better. Such cases are standard with 8mm and VHS-C tapes, but most VHS tapes come in an open-edge cardboard sleeve.

• Store tapes upright. If you lay them flat, gravity may deform them by exerting pressure on the tape edges.

• Choose a storage area that's well away from TV sets, loudspeakers, and other devices that give off strong magnetic or electrical fields.

- Store tapes where temperature and humidity are within moderate ranges—say, between 59°F and 77°F at 40–60 percent relative humidity. Never expose tapes to direct sunlight or leave them in a hot vehicle. If you move a tape to another location that's markedly different in temperature, allow the tape to acclimate for several hours before you play it.

- Seldom-played tapes should at least be "exercised" every year or two. Shuttling them through fast-forward and rewind cycles will prevent tape layers from sticking. If the recording shows signs of degradation, have it duplicated as soon as possible. A professional duplication center will yield the best-quality copies; look under "Video" in the Yellow Pages.

Recording speeds. Recording video at speeds slower than Standard Play (SP) is frugal and convenient. The Long Play recording speed doubles recording time compared with SP, whereas EP (sometimes called Super Long Play, or SLP) triples it. At the EP setting, then, you can squeeze six hours of recording time from a T120 tape.

However, VCRs generally show a decline in recording performance at EP compared with SP. Even LP recordings are usually noticeably poorer than those made at the fastest speed.

Vitamins

If you want to improve your health by increasing your vitamin intake, there is one strategy that no scientist would dispute: Eat more fruits and vegetables. These foods contain hundreds of substances that have the potential to improve health—not just the handful of compounds that have been isolated and packaged in pills. Moreover, a diet loaded with produce tends to be high in fiber and low in fat.

If you choose carefully—and eat five to nine servings of fruits and vegetables a day, as government guidelines now recommend—you can take in the relatively high levels of antioxidants that various studies have found to be protective. It's fairly easy to get 250–500 milligrams of vitamin C, which is abundant in oranges, cantaloupe, and peppers, among other foods. And selecting good sources of beta-carotene, such as sweet potatoes, apricots, and carrots, can add up to 10–15 milligrams (or 17,000–25,000 International Units a day).

Vitamin E poses more of a problem. With the exception of fortified cereals, the main dietary sources of vitamin E are polyunsaturated vegetable oils. You can get the U.S. Recommended Daily Allowance (RDA) for this vitamin fairly easily in a few tablespoons of sunflower oil, safflower oil, or mayonnaise. But to take in 100 to 400 IU, the amount used in many studies, would require eating a heavy dose of fatty foods or taking supplements.

If you decide to take vitamins, it pays to go for the bargain price. Products differ in some ways—some use "natural" ingredients, for example—but there isn't anything evident to justify the cost of high-priced brands.

Nutrients work together to allow the body to use them efficiently, so if you take a multiple supplement, choose one that provides about 100 percent of the U.S. RDA for all the vitamins and minerals for which an RDA has been set. That should be about all you need if you're taking vitamins simply as overall nutritional insurance. One important exception is calcium, which is too bulky to include in a multivitamin/mineral pill at the full U.S. RDA of 1,000 milligrams. If you need more calcium than you get in your diet, you'll need a separate calcium supplement.

If you have decided to take antioxidants (notably vitamins C and E and beta-carotene) for their possible health benefits, you can simply shop by price. Quality and cost seem unrelated.

For any nutritional supplement, look for an expiration date, which shows how long the supplement should retain its potency. (Vitamins break down over time; store them in a cool, dry place.)

W

Warehouse Clubs

If price and value are more important to you than variety, ambience, and service with a smile, consider joining a nearby warehouse club. Their prices are considerably lower—and in the case of big-ticket items, dramatically lower than those charged by competitors. Most supermarket-type products are sold in bulk sizes or multipacks. Such sizes are best suited to large families or to people with plenty of storage space.

Even if you'd rather shop for groceries at a supermarket, it may make sense to join a club if you're thinking of buying a TV set, exercise machine, or other fairly costly item. The savings on that single purchase could be enough to offset the annual membership fee.

If you're not sure about joining, visit the store, using a temporary pass. If you decide to sign up, here are a few shopping strategies:

- Avoid shopping on weekends, when checkout lines tend to be longest. Some stores bar consumer members until late morning on one or more days. That's to allow business customers to shop before their workday begins.

- Learn the store layout to avoid wasting time. Most clubs are divided into zones. For instance, food on one side; seasonal items, books, office supplies in the middle; and general merchandise, including linens, auto supplies, appliances, electronics, and housewares, on the other side.

• Keep price tags and receipts. Clubs typically offer full exchanges or refunds, but not without proof of purchase.

Washing Machines

Front-loader models are more expensive to buy than top-loaders. However, a front-loader's reduced operating costs—less detergent and fewer gallons of water to be heated—should make it cheaper in the long run than a top-loader.

Comparing the types. The familiar top-loading machine has important conveniences. Large-capacity models can handle as much as 14 pounds of laundry; a front-loader may not be able to handle more than about eight pounds. A top-loader's wash cycle is usually faster than a front-loader's. Unlike a front-loader, you can easily add items in the middle of a top-loader's wash cycle. However, for unbalanced loads the design of a front-loading machine allows for handling them easily. If floor space is tight, a front-loader, with a dryer on top, occupies a smaller area than a top-loader with a dryer alongside, and can fit into a small laundry nook.

Weather Radios

To help reduce the havoc caused by hurricanes, tornadoes, and other cataclysmic weather, the National Oceanic and Atmospheric Administration (NOAA) has established its own nationwide radio network to broadcast continuous weather information and warnings of impending weather emergencies.

The NOAA Weather Radio network, or NWR, can send out storm-watch messages hours in advance of a downpour or broadcast the first warning to a community about an impending tornado. A loud 10-second tone precedes emergency announcements.

The NWR broadcasts from more than 380 stations, on frequencies above the FM band. Each transmitter is designed to cover a 40-mile radius. Scanners, marine radios, and other specialized consumer equipment can receive the broadcasts. So can moderately priced weather-alert radios, which have one important feature most expensive equipment lacks: They can be left on in "alert" mode and play only when the NWR tone activates them.

Weather Stripping

Weather stripping, which blocks drafts around doors and windows, won't save much energy. Such drafts actually contribute little to overall heat loss. Still, weather stripping will do a lot to make a house feel more comfortable. That could save energy indirectly, since you may not need to turn up the thermostat as much if the room isn't drafty.

No single type of weather stripping works well everywhere. You'll probably need one type for doors, another for windows. The following descriptions can help you decide which type to use where; so can the instructions on the packaging.

Tape. EPDM (ethylene-propylene-diene monomer) rubber, nonporous closed-cell foam, open-cell foam, and sponge rubber. You can buy rolls of tape in various widths and thicknesses. The tape is self-adhesive and thus very easy to install. You cut the tape to length with scissors, peel away the backing and stick it in place.

Best uses: Along a doorjamb or at the top and bottom of a window sash. Tape works best when it's compressed. It's not well suited for a window jamb. The size and flexibility of tape make it well suited for blocking an irregular crack. Tape that's rectangular in cross sections is well suited for sealing corners.

Reinforced foam. Closed-cell foam tape attached to a strip of wood molding.

Best uses: Nailed in place around a window or doorjamb. Reinforced foam can be a bother to install.

Tension seal. A self-stick strip of plastic that's folded along its length to form a V, or a springy bronze strip that's shaped to bridge the gap between, say, a window sash and its frame. The shape of this type creates a seal by pressing against the sides of a crack to block drafts.

Best uses: Inside the track of a double-hung window or between a door and its jamb. Plastic V strips are easier to install than bronze. Either type can be hard to install in a corner.

Felt. Plain or reinforced with a flexible metal strip, sold in rolls that you cut to length and staple or tack in place. Felt seals best if you position the staples parallel to the length of the strip.

Best uses: Plain felt can be fitted in a doorjamb, so the door presses against it; reinforced felt can seal around a door or window.

Pile. A narrow strip of furry, carpetlike material with a rigid back. Some versions come with an adhesive backing.

Best uses: Fitted in recessed slots around the perimeter of a window sash, storm door, or sliding glass patio door.

Tubular rubber and vinyl. Tubes of sponge rubber or vinyl, with a flange along their length that you staple or tack in place. These gaskets work best when a door or window presses against them to form a seal. They aren't as easy to install as self-stick types.

Best use: Around a door.

Reinforced silicone. A tubular gasket attached to a metal strip, similar in appearance to reinforced tubular vinyl. It seals well but can be hard to install.

Best uses: On a doorjamb or window stop.

Door seals. These seal the space beneath a door. An effective variety is a vinyl door seal with multiple sealing edges of equal length. This type outperforms felt and brush seals. The ones with an adhesive backing are especially easy to install.

Windows, Replacement

There's no point in spending thousands of dollars for new windows just to cut your energy bills. Even purchasing the best replacement windows would result in only a modest drop in heating and cooling costs. But you may need new windows if you've remodeled or because the frames have deteriorated. Then it makes sense to choose durable windows that keep out wind and water and that offer high thermal performance.

Frames

Wood frames, plain or clad in vinyl or aluminum, tend to be more expensive than all-vinyl. Plain wood, of course, needs to be painted. Clad wood requires minimal maintenance.

Aluminum is a good heat conductor. Even an aluminum-framed window that is "thermally broken," with insulation between the interior and exterior parts, conducts more heat than vinyl- or wood-frame windows. In cold weather, heat inside the house travels readily through the frame to the out-doors, making the indoor side of the window feel cold to the touch. In a temperate climate an aluminum frame may be a practical choice, but it won't offer the best thermal protection in cold New England winters.

Better-quality vinyl windows have welded corners. Other windows may have corners that are screwed together. Avoid such windows. They're less likely to be airtight and watertight, and the corners may start to pull apart after being exposed to heat and cold.

Glass

Single-pane. In cold climates and hot ones, single-pane windows are best reserved for garages and other spaces that don't require heating or cooling. But single-panes may be adequate in areas with brief heating and air-conditioning seasons.

Double-pane. Most new homes have this type. It consists of two sealed panes, usually separated by an aluminum spacer that includes a desiccant to keep moisture from condensing between the panes. Once that happens, the only way to get rid of moisture is to replace the glass.

Argon-filled. In a regular double-glazed window, air fills the gap between the panes. A step up in thermal performance and price are windows filled with an inert gas, usually argon. Argon-filled glazing achieves its optimum performance with a half-inch space between panes; air-filled windows perform best with a space of one-half to one inch.

Y

Yogurt

Yogurt, as long as it's either low-fat or no-fat, is a nutritious and healthy food and an excellent source of calcium and protein. Some people find it easier to digest if it contains live *Lactobacillus bulgaricus* or *Streptococcus thermophilus* bacteria, and there's some evidence that eating live *Lactobacillus acidophilus* bacteria helps women prevent vaginal yeast infections. Other than that, health claims made for live bacteria in yogurt have not been borne out by medical studies.

Index

A

Accident insurance, 203
Acidophilus milk, 142
AIDS, 189
Air bags, facial injuries from, 3
Air conditioners, 3–4
Airplane travel,
  seating strategy for, 4–5
Alarms, burglar, 30–32
Alkaline batteries, 20
Alpha-hydroxy acids (AHAs), 143
Aluminum foil, 96–97
American Express
  traveler's checks, 202
American National Standards
  Institute (ANSI), 20, 21
American Society for Testing and
  Materials (ASTM), 20, 21
Annual Fuel Utilization Efficiency
  rating (AFUE), 100, 101
Annuities, variable, 206
Answering machines, 190–91
Antacids, 37
Antidepressants, 189
Antifreeze, 176
Antihistamines, 189
Antihypertensives, 189
Antiquarian Booksellers
  Association, 60
Antispasmodics, 189
Apparel, See Clothing
Appliances
  can openers, 40
  clothes dryers, 45, 75
  dishwashers, 63–64
  electric ranges, 72–73
  energy conservation, 74
  gas ranges, 109–11
  microwave ovens, 140–42
  mixers, food, 95–96
  pressure cookers, 153
  ranges, 72–73, 109–11
  refrigerators, See Refrigerators
  repairing, 158–61
  steam irons, 180
  toaster-oven broilers, 194–95
  toasters, 195
  washing machines, 74–75, 212
"As is" purchases, 168
Aspirin, 6–7
Association of Home Appliance
  Manufacturers, 75
AT&T, 137, 192
ATM use when traveling, 202–203
Automatic teller machines
  (ATMs), 202–203
Autombile Association of America
  (AAA), 202
Automobile loans, 10
  balloon loans, 10–11
Automobile rentals
  extras, 11–13
  fuel charges, 13
Automobiles
  batteries, 7–8, 14
  battery booster cables, 9–10
  energy conservation measures, 75
  hazardous automotive
    products, 112–13
  international driving, 128–29
  jack stands, 131
  jump–starting, 9–10
  loans, See Automobile loans
  rentals, See Automobile rentals
  repairs while on the road, 13–14

tires, 13, 14–16
  used, prices of, 14
  warranties, 16–17
  washing and polishing, 17–19

B

Baby food, pesticides in, 151
Balloon loans, automobile, 10–11
Batteries, 20
  alkaline, 20
  automobile, 7–8, 14
  booster cables for automobile, 9–10
  nickel-cadmium, 20
Beta-blockers, 127
Beverages
  caffeine in, See Caffeine
  coffee, See Coffee
  iced tea, 124
  milk, acidophilus, 142
  orange juice, 148
  wine, sulfites in, 183
  See also Food
Bicycles, 21–22
  casual, 21–22
  helmets, 20–21
  mountain, 22
  stationary, 79–80
Birth-control pills, gum disease in
  women taking, 188
Blankets, electric, 71–72
Bleaches, 133
Bonds
  rating grades, 23
  zero-coupon, 198
Boom boxes, 23–24
Borrowing instead of buying
  a product, 33
Bread, 24–27
  breadmakers, 27–29
  commercially prepared,
    ingredients added to, 26–27
  dating of, 27
  as fiber source, 25, 26, 88
  nutritional value of, 24, 25–26
  rye, 25
  spreads for, 29–30
  storing to maintain freshness, 27
  white, 25
  whole wheat, 25, 88

Breadmakers, 27–29
Bread spreads, 29–30
Burglar alarms, 30–32
Butter, 29–30
Buying advice, general, 32–33

C

Caffeine, 34–36
  in brewed versus instant coffee, 34
  in decaffeinated coffee, 34
  in "half-caf," 34
  health risks of, 35–36, 115
  in products other than
    coffee, 36, 115
Calcium in the diet, 36–37
  supplements to, 37
Calorie budgeting, 37
Camcorders, 38
Cameras, 38–39
  autoexposure, 38–39
  film for, 89–90
  single-lens reflex (SLR), 39
Cancer, 87, 175
  skin, 183
Can openers, 39–40
Carbon monoxide detectors, 40–41
Cars, See Automobiles
Catalog shopping, 150
  Federal Trade Commission
    rule, 168–69
CD players, 41–42
CD-ROM, computer, 51
Central heating, 74
Ceramides, 143
Cereal
  as fiber source, 88
  prices of, 42
Certified Financial Planners, 146
Charge cards, See Credit cards
Checks, liability for stolen, 180–81
Chicken soup, 177, 178
Children
  baby food, pesticides in, 151
  bicycle helmets for, 21
  insect repellent used on, 126
  solvent exposure, preventing, 176
  strep infection, 181
  strollers for, 182–83
Chips and dips, 62–63

Chocolate chip cookies, 42–44
Cholesterol, 85, 87, 88
Christmas trees, 44
Clinton, Hillary Rodham, chocolate
    chip cookie recipe, 43
Clothes dryers, 45, 75
Clothing
    private-label, 6
    shoes, *See* Shoes
    shopping strategies, 5–6
    sweaters, 185–86
Coats, buying winter, 5
Coffee
    beans, 46
    brewed, 34, 45–46
    caffeine content of, *See* Caffeine
    preserving freshness, 45–46
Coffeemakers, 46–48
    brewing, 47–48
    capacity of, 47
    cleanup, 48
    the French press, 48
    loading, 47
    manual drip, 48
    percolators, 48
Cold, common, 50
Collagen, 144
Collision-damage waiver (CDW), 12
Comforters, 49–50
Common cold, 50
Comparison shopping, 33
Computers
    buying, 50–51
    CD-ROM, 51
    fax/modem, 51
    hard drive, 51
    monitor, 50–51
    plug and play, 51
    printers, 52–53
    processor, 51
    software, 51
    sound card, 51
    surge suppressors for, 185
    Windows software, 51
Condoms, 53–54
Conservation of energy, 73–75,
    156–57, 170, 193, 213–15
Consumer Price Index (CPI), 68

Consumer Product Safety
    Commission (CPSC), 103
Contact lenses, "extended wear," 82
Containers, plastic food, 98
Cookies, chocolate chip, 42–44
Cordless drills, 153
Cordless telephones, 54–55
Credit cards, 55–58
    accident insurance, 203
    annual fees, 55
    ATM use with, 202–203
    bank cards versus store cards, 5
    card registries, 56–57
    cash advances, 57
    for consolidating debt, 55
    Fair Credit Billing Act protection
        for purchases with, 169–70
    fraud protection, 56–57
    grace period, 55
    interest charges, 33
    interest rates, 55, 56
    line of credit, 56
    lost or stolen, 56–57
    number to use, 57–58
    paying off balance on, 120
    paying the full bill monthly, 33
    tricks and traps, 57
Cribs, 58–59
    hand-me-downs, 58–59
    mattresses for, 59

D

Decaffeinated coffee, 34–35
Declaration of Independence, 60
Decongestants, 127, 189
Deet, 125–26
Dehumidifiers, 60–61
Dehydration, 61
Department of Agriculture, U.S., 29
Depression, 62
    impotence and, 124, 125
Detergents, 133
    concentrated laundry, 133
    dishwater, 63
    laundry, 133
Diabetes, 189
Digestion, caffeine and, 36
Dips and chips, 62–63

Dishwashers, 63–64
  detergents for, 63
Dividend-reinvestment programs, 129
Doctor-patient relationship, 65
Dollar, strong or weak, 69
Doors
  energy conservation measures, 73
  garage door openers, 103–105
  locks, 65–67
  weather stripping, 213–15
Down comforters, 49
  synthetic, 50
Drain cleaning, 67
Dress shoes, 165–66
Drills, power, 152–53

E

Economic statistics, 68–69
Eggs, 70–71
Elastin, 144
Electric blankets
  and mattress pads, 71–72
Electric ranges, 72–73
  gas burners, 73
Energy conservation, 73–75, 156–57,
  170, 193, 213–15
Exchange rates, 202–203
Exercise
  during the day, 76
  hydration, 61
  machines, *See* Exercise machines
  during the winter, 76–77
Exercise machines, 77–81
  assembly of, 77–78
  ski machines, 78–79
  stair climbers, 80–81
  stationary bicycles, 79–80
  treadmills, 78
  trying out before purchasing, 77
Extended warranties, 17, 81, 120
"Extended wear" contact lenses, 82
Eyesight, conditions that may
  damage, 82

F

Facial moisturizers, 142–44
Fair Credit Billing Act, 169–70
Family Circle bake-off, 43

Fast food, 83–84
Fats, 84–85
  in bread spreads, 29–30
  in fast foods,
    minimizing intake of, 83–84
  fat-free foods, 84
  in ice cream, 123
  low-fat foods, 24, 84
  monounsaturated, 84–85
  in peanut butter, 150
  in peanuts, 150
  polyunsaturated, 84, 85
  saturated, 84, 85, 123
Fax machines, 85–87
  computer fax/modems, 51
  features of, 86–87
  paper for, 86
Federal Trade Commission, 140
  "Cooling Off Rule," 169
  "Mail Order Rule," 168–69
Feminine hygiene pads, 187–88
Fiber, 87–89
  in bread, 25, 26
  in peanut butter, 150
Film, 89–90
Financial planners, 145–46
Fire extinguishers, 90–93
  choosing, 92
  safety check, 92–93
  types of, 91–92
  types of fires, 90–91
Fish, buying, 93–94
Fish oil, 199
Fluoridated mouthwash, 144
Fluoridated water and toothpaste, 189
FM receivers, 154
Food
  baby food, pesticides in, 151
  bread, *See* Bread
  calcium in, *See* Calcium in the
    diet
  cereal prices, 42
  containers and wraps, 96–98
  cookies, chocolate chip, 42–44
  fast food, 83–84
  fats in, *See* Fats
  fiber in, *See* Fiber
  fish, buying, 93–94

frozen yogurt, 123–24
ice cream, 123–24
ices, 124
labeling of, 94–95, 123
low-oxalate, 132
mixers, 95–96
oranges, 148
peanut butter, 150
peanuts, 150
salmon, canned, 199
salsa, 162–63
sherbets, 124
soups, 177–79
stir-frying, 180
tomatoes, 196
tuna canned in oil, 199
turkey, 199–200
vegetable nutrition, 206–207
wraps and containers, 96–98
See also Beverages
Food and Drug Administration, U.S.,
    29, 35, 36, 94, 95, 117
Food-storage bags, 97–98
Foreign exchange, 202–203
401(k) plans, 129
Fragrances, 98–99
Freezer bags, 97–98
French press coffeemakers, 48
Frozen yogurt, 123–24
Furnaces, 74, 99–102
    installation, choosing a company
        for, 101–102
    maintenance contract for, 102
    price of efficiency, 101
    replacing, 100
    tuneup, 99–100

G
Games and toys, 196–97
Garage door openers, 103–105
Garbage bags, 105–106
Garbage disposers, 106–109
    batch-feed, 107, 108
    continuous-feed, 107–108
    installation, 109
    jams, 108
    materials not to put down, 108–109
    splashing, 109

Gas cooktops, 73
Gas ranges, 109–11
Glasses, reading, 82
Glue, 111
Glycol ethers, 176–77
Gross domestic product (GDP), 69
Gum disease, 188–89

H
Halogen lamps, 112
Hands, smelly, 112
Hard drive, computer, 51
Hazardous waste at home, 112–14
Health insurance, 203
Heartbeat, caffeine and
    irregular, 35–36
Heartburn, 114–15
Heart disease, 87, 88
Heaters
    furnaces, *See* Furnaces
    portable, 115–16
Helmets, bicycle, 20–21
Herbal supplements, 116–17
*Herbs of Choice—The Therapeutic Use
    of Phytomedicinals* (Tyler), 116
High blood pressure, caffeine
    consumption and, 35–36
High-density lipoproteins (HDLs), 85
Holiday blues, 62
Home, shopping at, 169
Homeowner's insurance, 117–19,
    162, 203
Home robberies
    burglar alarms, 30–32
    preventive measures, 30–31
Home theater, 119–20
*Honest Herbal—a Sensible Guide to the
    Use of Herbs and Related
    Remedies, The* (Tyler), 116
Hotel security, 120–21
Household cleaners, disposal of
    hazardous, 112–14
Humidifiers, 121–22
Hypothermia, 76–77

I
Ice cream, 123–24
Iced tea, 124

Ices, 124
Implied warranties, 168
Impotence, 124–25
Index of leading economic
    indicators, 69
Insect repellents, 125–27
Insomnia, 127
Insurance
    accident, 203
    cancellation of policy, 128
    health, 203
    homeowner's, 117–19, 162, 203
    liability, *See* Liability insurance
    safe-deposit box, 162
    travel, 203
    variable annuities, 206
International driving, 128–29
International Driving Permit
    (IDP), 128
Investing
    counseling, 145–46
    $50 or less, 129–30
    in mutual funds, 145–46
    in Treasury securities, 198
    variable annuities, 206
Irons, 180

J

Jack stands, 131
*Journal of the American Medical
    Association*, 36

K

Kidney stones, 132
Knives, pocket, 151–52

L

Labeling of food, 94–95, 123
Lamps, halogen, 112
Laundry detergents, 133
Lawn blowers, 134
Lawn mowers, 134–36
    electric, 135
    gas, 135
    manual, 135
    mulch, 135–36
    tips on using, 134

Legal rights of shoppers, *See*
    Shopping rights
Liability insurance
    automobile rentals and, 12–13
Light bulbs, 75
Lighting, 75
Liposomes, 143
Lipstick, 136
Loans
    automobile, *See* Automobile loans
    no-income-verification, 136–37
    for self-employed, 136–37
Locks, door, 65–67
Long-distance calls, 137
Loudspeakers, 137–38
Low-density lipoproteins (LDLs), 85
Luggage
    soft-sided, 138–39
    stolen, 203
Lung disease and exposure to
    solvents, 175
Lyme disease, 126–27

M

Mail-order shopping, 140
    Federal Trade Commission rule,
        168–69
Manual drip coffeemakers, 48
Margarine, 29–30
Mattresses
    crib, 59
    electric mattress pads, 71–72
MCI, 192
Medical emergencies when
    traveling, 203
Methylene chloride, 34, 35, 175, 176
Microwave ovens, 140–41
    produce cooked in, 142
Milk, acidophilus, 142
Miscarriage, caffeine and, 35
Mixers, food, 95–96
Moisturizers, facial, 142–44
Money-market mutual funds, 145
Monounsaturated fats, 84–85
Mortgages, prepaying, 129–30
Mountain bikes, 22
Mouthwash, fluoridated, 144
Mulch, 135–36

Muscle relaxants, 189
Muscle sprains, 144
Mutual funds, 145–46

N

Nail care, 147
National Academy of Sciences, 151
National Archives, 60
National Institute
of Mental Health, 62
National Mental Health
Association, 62
National Oceanic and
Atmospheric Administration
(NOAA) Weather Radio
network, 212–13
New product, determining your
need for, 32
N-Hexane, 177
Nickel-cadmium batteries, 20
No-income-verification loans, 136–37
Nursing women, 117

O

Omega-3 fatty acids, 199
1,1,1 trichloroethane, 176
Oranges and orange juice, 148
Osteoporosis, 37
Oxalates in the diet, 132

P

Paints, 176
disposal of, 113, 114
interior latex, 149–50
Paper wraps, 97
Peanut butter, 150
Peanuts, 150
Penn State Center for Sports
Medicine, 76–77
Percolators, 48
Perfume, 98–99
Permethrin, 126
Pesticides, 113, 177
in baby food, 151
Petroleum distillates, 177
Plastic containers, 98
Plastic wrap, 97

Plug and play, 51
Pneumonia vaccination, 151
Pocket knives, 151–52
Polishing nails, 147
Polyunsaturated fats, 84, 85
Portable heaters, 115–16
Power drills, 152–53
Pregnant women
caffeine and, 35
condoms to prevent
pregnancy, 53–54
gum disease and, 188
herbal supplements and, 117
solvent exposure, 175
Prepaying your mortgage, 129–30
Pressure cookers, 153
Pricey product, determining your
need for, 32
Printers, computer, 52–53
Producer Price Index (PPI), 68
Public resources, making use of, 33

R

Ramen, 179
Reading glasses, 82
Real estate, time-share, 193–94
Receivers, 154
Refrigerators, 154–57
energy-efficient operation
of, 74, 156–57
features, 156
types of, 155
Remote controls, 157–58
Renting
automobiles,
See Automobile rentals
instead of buying a product, 33
Repairing
of appliances, 158–61
versus replacing a product, 32
Replacement windows, 215–16
Rights, shopping,
See Shopping rights
Robberies, preventing, 30–32
Rolaids, 37
Rollerblading, 161
Running shoes, 166
Rye bread, 25

S

Saber saws, 163
Safe-deposit box insurance, 162
Salmon, canned, 199
Salsa, 162–63
Sanitary napkins, 187–88
Saturated fats, 84, 85, 123
Savings Bonds, Series EE, 129
Saws, saber, 163
Screwdrivers, 164–65
Security
    home systems, 31–32
    hotel, 120–21
Self-employed, loans for, 136–37
Sharing instead of
    buying a product, 33
Sherbets, 124
Shoes
    dress, 165–66
    running, 166
Shopping channels on TV, 167
Shopping rights, 168–70
    catalog shopping, 168–69
    credit card purchases, 169–70
    at-home shopping, 169
    warranties, See Warranties
Showerheads, 170
Ski machines, 78–79
Sleep difficulties, 127
Smelly hands, 112
Smoke detectors, 171–73
Smoking
    gum disease and, 188–89
    quitting at 65, 173
Snell Memorial Foundation, 20, 21
Soaps, 173–74
Soft drinks, caffeine in, 36
Software, 51
Solvent hazards, 113, 175–77
    common organic solvents, 176–77
    disposal of solvents, 113
    reducing exposure, 175–76
Sound card, computer, 51
Soups, 177–79
Spackling, 179
Sprains, muscle, 144
Spreads, bread, 29–30
Sprint, 192

Stair climbers, 80–81
Standard & Poor's, 23
Stationary bicycles, 79–80
Steam irons, 180
Stereo receivers, 154
Stir-frying, 180
Stocks
    dividend-reinvestment
        programs, 129
    mutual funds, 145–46
Stolen checks, liability for, 180–81
Stolen credit cards, 56–57
Strep infection in children, 181
Strollers, 182–83
Sulfites in wine, 183
Sunscreens, 183–84
Surge suppressors
    for computers, 185
Surround receivers, 154
Sweaters, 185–86
Swimmer's ear, 186
Swimsuits, 5
Synthetic down comforters, 50
Synthetic fill comforters, 49–50

T

Tampons, 187
Tape decks, 188
Tea, iced, 124
Teeth
    gum disease, 188–89
    preventing decay, 189
    sealants, 189, 190
    sensitivity, 189–90
Telephones
    answering machines, 190–91
    calling cards, 137
    cordless, 54–55
    long–distance calls, 137
    rates, 192
    voice mail, 191
Television, See TV
Thermostats, energy-saving, 73, 193
Ticks, 126–27
Time-share real estate, 193–94
Tires, automobile, 13, 14–16
Toaster-oven broilers, 194–95
Toasters, 195

Toilet tanks, water-saving measures for, 195–96
Toll House cookies, original, 43–44
Toluene, 175, 176
Tomatoes, 196
Tomato vegetable soup, 177, 178
Tools
  saber saws, 163
  screwdrivers, 164–65
Toothpaste
  desensitizing, 189–90
  fluoridated, 189
Toys and games, 196–97
Tranquilizers, 189
Trash bags, 105–106
Trash compactors, 197–98
Travel
  by air, seating strategy for, 4–5
  automobile repairs, 13–14
  vacation money, 202–203
Traveler's checks, 202
Travel insurance, 203
Treadmills, 77
Treasury securities, 198
Trees, 74
  Christmas, 44
Trip-cancellation insurance, 203
Tums, 37
Tuna canned in oil, 199
Turkey, 199–200
TV
  sets, 192–93
  shopping channels, 167
  /VCR combinations, 201
Tyler, Varro, 116

U
Underwriter Laboratories (UL), 185
Unemployment rate, 68–69
U.S. Savings Bonds, 129
Used cars, 14

V
Vacations
  money for, 202–203
  planning, 204
Vacuum cleaners, 205–206
Variable annuities, 206

VCRs, 207
  \TV combinations, 201
Vegetable nutrition, 206–207
Videocassette recorders (VCRs), 207
  \TV combinations, 201
Videotape, 208–209
Vitamin C, 210
Vitamin D, 184
Vitamin E, 210
Vitamins, 209–10
  storage of, 210
Voice mail, 191

W
Warehouse clubs, 211–12
Warranties, 168
  automobile, 16–17
  extended, 17, 81, 120
  implied, 168
Washing machines, 74–75, 212
Water heaters, 74
Weather radios, 212–13
Weather stripping, 213–15
Weight loss, 84
White bread, 25
Whole wheat bread, 25, 88
Windows
  energy conservation measures, 73
  replacement, 215–16
  weather stripping, 213–15
Windows software, 51
Wine, sulfites in, 183

Y
Yeast infections, 217
Yogurt, 217
  frozen, 123–24

Z
Zero-coupon bonds, 198